PORCHES
AND PATIOS

Other Publications:

TRUE CRIME
THE AMERICAN INDIANS
THE ART OF WOODWORKING
LOST CIVILIZATIONS
ECHOES OF GLORY
THE NEW FACE OF WAR
HOW THINGS WORK
WINGS OF WAR
CREATIVE EVERYDAY COOKING
COLLECTOR'S LIBRARY OF THE UNKNOWN
CLASSICS OF WORLD WAR II
TIME-LIFE LIBRARY OF CURIOUS AND UNUSUAL FACTS
AMERICAN COUNTRY
VOYAGE THROUGH THE UNIVERSE
THE THIRD REICH
THE TIME-LIFE GARDENER'S GUIDE
MYSTERIES OF THE UNKNOWN
TIME FRAME
FIX IT YOURSELF
FITNESS, HEALTH & NUTRITION
SUCCESSFUL PARENTING
HEALTHY HOME COOKING
UNDERSTANDING COMPUTERS
LIBRARY OF NATIONS
THE ENCHANTED WORLD
THE KODAK LIBRARY OF CREATIVE PHOTOGRAPHY
GREAT MEALS IN MINUTES
THE CIVIL WAR
PLANET EARTH
COLLECTOR'S LIBRARY OF THE CIVIL WAR
THE EPIC OF FLIGHT
THE GOOD COOK
WORLD WAR II
THE OLD WEST

For information on and a full description of any of the
Time-Life Books series listed above, please call
1-800-621-7026 or write:
Reader Information
Time-Life Customer Service
P.O. Box C-32068
Richmond, Virginia 23261-2068

This volume is part of a series offering homeowners
detailed instructions on repairs, construction and
improvements they can undertake themselves.

HOME REPAIR
AND IMPROVEMENT

PORCHES AND PATIOS

BY THE EDITORS OF
TIME-LIFE BOOKS

TIME-LIFE BOOKS
ALEXANDRIA, VIRGINIA

TIME-LIFE BOOKS

Editor-in-Chief	Thomas H. Flaherty
Director of Editorial Resources	Elise D. Ritter-Clough
Executive Art Director	Ellen Robling
Director of Photography and Research	John Conrad Weiser
Editorial Board	Dale M. Brown, Janet Cave, Roberta Conlan, Robert Doyle, Laura Foreman, Jim Hicks, Rita Thievon Mullin, Henry Woodhead
Assistant Director of Editorial Resources	Norma E. Shaw
President	John D. Hall
Vice President and Director of Marketing	Nancy K. Jones
Editorial Director	Lee Hassig
Director of Production Services	Robert N. Carr
Production Manager	Marlene Zack
Supervisor of Quality Control	James King

Editorial Operations

Production	Celia Beattie
Library	Louise D. Forstall
Computer Composition	Deborah G. Tait (Manager), Monika D. Thayer, Janet Barnes Syring, Lillian Daniels
Interactive Media Specialist	Patti H. Cass

Time-Life Books is a division of
Time Life Incorporated

President and CEO	John M. Fahey, Jr.

HOME REPAIR AND IMPROVEMENT

Editorial Staff for *Porches and Patios*

Editor	Robert M. Jones
Assistant Editors	Betsy Frankel, Brooke Stoddard
Designer	Edward Frank
Picture Editor	Adrian Allen
Associate Designer	Kenneth E. Hancock
Text Editors	William Worsley (senior), Lynn R. Addison, Peter Pocock
Staff Writers	Patricia C. Bangs, Jan Leslie Cook, Carol J. Corner, Rachel Cox, Robert A. Doyle, Steven J. Forbis, Kathleen M. Kiely, Victoria W. Monks, Ania Savage, Mary-Sherman Willis
Researcher	Kimberly K. Lewis
Art Associates	George Bell, Fred Holz, Lorraine D. Rivard
Editorial Assistant	Susan Larson
Special Contributor	Lydia Preston (text)

Editorial Production

Production Editor	Douglas B. Graham
Operations Manager	Gennaro C. Esposito, Gordon E. Buck (assistant)
Assistant Production Editor	Feliciano Madrid
Quality Control	Robert L. Young (director), James J. Cox (assistant), Daniel J. McSweeney, Michael G. Wight (associates)
Art Coordinator	Anne B. Landry
Copy Staff	Susan B. Galloway (chief), Margery duMond, Diane Ullius Jarrett, Celia Beattie
Picture Department	Betsy Donahue
Traffic	Jeanne Potter

Correspondents: Elisabeth Kraemer-Singh (Bonn); Margot Hapgood, Dorothy Bacon, Lesley Coleman, Patricia Vaughn (London); Susan Jonas, Lucy T. Voulgaris (New York); Maria Vincenza Aloisi, Josephine du Brusle (Paris); Ann Natanson (Rome). Valuable assistance was also provided by: Judy Aspinall, Karin B. Pearce (London); Carolyn T. Chubet, Miriam Hsia, Christina Lieberman (New York); Mimi Murphy (Rome).

THE CONSULTANTS: Roswell W. Ard is a consulting structural engineer and a professional home inspector in northern Michigan. He has written professionally on the structural uses of wood and on wood-frame construction techniques, and is experienced in finish carpentry.

Robert K. Crosby has been a general contractor and custom builder for more than a decade. His particular interests include building Cape Cod and Colonial houses and working with concrete and tile.

Ronald V. Croy has worked in the contracting business for more than two decades and operated his own firm for eight years. He is an expert in carpentry and specializes in remodeling residential structures.

Harris Mitchell, special consultant for Canada, has worked in the field of home repair and improvement for more than two decades. He is Homes editor of *Today* magazine and author of a syndicated newspaper column, as well as a number of books on home improvement.

David Thompson is former president of a contracting firm that built subdivisions and custom homes. He has also worked in the restoration of Victorian-era townhouses and is foreman for a construction company in Springfield, Virginia.

Richard VanCamp is president of a contracting firm that specializes in designing and constructing decks.

John Wiebenson is principal architect for Wiebenson and Associates, for which he designs residential, commercial and institutional structures. He has taught architecture at Yale University and the University of Maryland and is a frequent lecturer at the Smithsonian Institution in Washington, D.C.

Library of Congress Cataloguing in Publication Data
Time-Life Books.
    Porches and patios.
    (Home repair and improvement; 26)
    Includes index.
    1. Porches—Amateurs' manuals. 2. Patios—Amateurs' manuals.
    I. Title.
TH4970.T55   1981   690'.184   80-25864
ISBN 0-8094-3476-8
ISBN 0-8094-3475-X (lib. bdg.)
ISBN 0-8094-3474-1 (retail ed.)

Contents

Making the Outdoors Habitable

Surrogate support. A telescoping house jack shores up a section of porch roof while a weakened column is replaced. Though apparently solid, the column is actually a decorative shell encasing a wood post. The jack is rentable, and column manufacturers mill the two-part enclosures in a wide variety of styles, including a choice of plinths and pediments.

The urge to live in the open air comes as naturally to people as their urge to seek shelter, and architectural history abounds in examples of ways to satisfy both. Two classical approaches, the porch and the patio, have long been part of the American scene, and—with a recent variation, the deck—are common appendages to modern homes.

Each kind of structure differs substantially from the others in form as well as in spirit. A porch is a roofed structure attached to the house, often at a point of entrance. It may have a concrete floor, but more commonly it has a wood floor that very much resembles the tongue-and-groove flooring on the inside of the house. The floorboards rest on joists supported by masonry piers.

Patios and decks are essentially open-air structures, although they may have some sort of rudimentary sun screen. A patio is a masonry platform set at ground level, and it can be formal or informal, depending on the materials used. Bricks set in sand, or concrete pavers sunk in gravel, are considerably more casual than an elegantly veneered surface of ceramic tiles. Decks are deliberately informal. Built of wood and often left unfinished, they are meant for rustic settings and hard use and are frequently chosen for rough terrains.

In planning an outdoor living area, it is important to consider not only design but also cost and comfort. Tile is by far the most expensive surfacing material—costing, with its concrete base, more than twice as much as a plain concrete slab and three times as much as bricks set in sand. For a deck, the cost of materials is approximately half that of a comparably sized porch; but if you add a sun screen, the deck's price will rise close to that of a porch.

The desire for comfort requires taking into account such things as orientation and prevailing winds. In most parts of the United States and southern Canada a porch, patio or deck on the north side of the house will be in shade most of the day; a southern exposure will provide bright morning light; a southwestern exposure will get late-afternoon sun. Similarly, although strong winds sweeping across a deck can spoil it for sun-bathing, gentle breezes can make open-air relaxation more pleasurable.

Planning will also involve checking to make sure the new facility does not interfere with utility lines—water, gas, sewage, telephone—and that it conforms to local building codes. Porches and decks are subject to many more restrictions than patios because they often are structural adjuncts to the house. In many localities you may not build closer than 25 feet to the front and rear property lines or closer than 5 to 15 feet to the side lines. To avoid last-minute disappointments, it is a good idea to draw up a rough sketch of your proposed plan and show it to the authorities before you begin.

A Spacious Porch with a Choice of Views

An L-shaped wraparound porch, favorite of Teddy Roosevelt's day, has much to recommend it. Not only does it soften the lines of a house, but it offers two different views, two different exposures, and two distinct types of outdoor activity. From the front you can watch the world go by, see and be seen; on the side you can withdraw from the world, watch the birds and read a book.

Constructing a porch that rounds the corner of a house is a major undertaking, involving concrete footings and brick piers below the floor, plus railings, columns and a shingled hip roof above it. Building codes inevitably loom large in its design. Check your local codes, which may restrict the square footage of developed space allowed on your property, as well as setback requirements dictating how close you may build to the street, to a neighbor's property and to underground utility lines. Codes may also require that, before you build, you treat the site to prevent termites.

These preliminaries taken care of, draw a plan of the porch, scaled to the size and shape of your house. A large house, for example, can handle a porch that spans two entire sides, but a small house would be engulfed by such a porch.

Most porch floors are 8 to 10 feet deep if designed to hold furniture, and lie one step—about 6 to 7½ inches—below the level of the house floor. Supporting the porch floor are evenly spaced piers that should be positioned so that they—and the posts or columns that sit directly above them to support the roof—will frame rather than block doors and windows. A broad flight of stairs, at least 8 feet wide for a large porch, should lead onto the porch in line with a door.

The site may need some work before construction can begin. If your property slopes more than 3 feet in 8, have a professional excavator do the necessary grading. Concrete steps or sidewalks, if you have them, may also need to be removed. For large demolition projects, you can rent a jackhammer; for smaller jobs, use a 10-pound sledge.

Once the site is prepared, you are ready to begin building. The first step is to cut away a strip of siding along the walls the porch will span, just above the foundation, exposing the sheathing or header joist beneath. The top of the exposed area should be ¼ inch above the planned height of the porch floor.

Then lay out the porch perimeter, using stakes and mason's cord (a stiff kind of string). Square corners are essential; they are obtained by the 3-4-5 method of triangulation, in which two steel-tape rulers are fastened to the house wall to form a right triangle whose sides are multiples of 3, 4 and 5 (opposite, bottom).

Outside the porch boundary lines, build a line of batter boards for reference in planning the height of the brick piers that will support the porch floor. For drainage, these piers should allow the porch floor to slope slightly away from the house—1 inch in 8 feet. To establish this slope, use a water level—a length of transparent garden hose filled with water. This ingenious tool is ideal for marking level lines over long distances because the water remains at the same height at both ends of the hose, no matter how irregular the terrain in between.

When the layout is completed, the foundation for the porch is prepared. The size, depth and spacing of concrete footings are determined by local codes according to the climate, the soil type and the load that the foundation must support. The load is expressed in terms of pounds per square foot (psf). For a calculated load of 60 psf (50 psf for live load, such as people, plus 10 psf for dead load, the weight of the porch structure), footings with dimensions 4 inches greater than the piers they support are adequate.

To calculate how much concrete you need, multiply the area of one footing by its depth in feet, and divide by 27 to get the volume in cubic yards. Then multiply this figure by the number of footings to get the total volume. If the total is less than 1 cubic yard, buy the concrete premixed in bags; order larger amounts from a transit-mix company (page 68).

The brick piers that rise above the footings should be built with standard construction-grade cored bricks. These come with one smooth side, which is laid facing outward, for a more finished look. Using a premixed mortar of cement, lime and sand (page 80) will simplify the construction of the piers; one cubic foot of mortar will bond 25 to 30 bricks.

The easiest way to figure the number of bricks you need is with a mason's rule, a folding ruler marked in inches on one side and in courses—or layers—of brick, tile and concrete block on the other. Once you have determined the planned height of the pier—which should reach from just below grade to the bottom of the porch floor joists—use the mason's rule to determine how many courses of brick you will need. Multiply that number by the number of bricks per course (page 11, Step 1) and again by the number of piers, for the grand total. To this total figure add 5 per cent, for waste.

To build the brick piers, you will need a pointed mason's trowel for spreading mortar, and a jointer—a narrow metal tool with a convex edge that is pressed into the wet mortar joints to shape and smooth them.

Over the brick piers lies a substructure of joists and band beams to support the porch floor. The chart on page 12 gives the maximum spans for various joist dimensions; but in general a porch that is 8 feet deep, like the one shown here, is supported by 2-by-8 joists spaced 16 inches apart. Use a strong wood, such as Douglas fir or southern pine, that has been pressure-treated.

To build this substructure, you will need two types of joist hangers—U-shaped hangers to connect the joists to the ledger board and L-shaped hangers, which can be bent to any angle, to install the end joists and the doubled joist that supports the porch corner. You will also need a hammer drill—a heavy-duty masonry drill that can be rented at a construction-tool-rental store—to drill holes for the bolts that fasten the ledger board to the house foundation.

Tongue-and-groove wood floorboards and the stock for the stairs should be treated with a wood preservative before they are nailed into place. You may want to rent a power nailer to make the job of installing floorboards go quickly. Once the floor and stairs are in place, you can add columns (page 29) or posts (pages 28-29), a railing (pages 28-29) and a roof (pages 18-28). When the porch is completed, paint the floor and stairs with a finish coat made for porches and decks.

Anatomy of a wraparound porch floor. The 8-foot-deep wraparound porch floor at right extends 40 feet along one entire side of the house and 18 feet along a perpendicular side. The floor, made of ¾-by-3¼-inch tongue-and-groove boards, rests atop a framework of 2-by-8 joists and beams. Full-length joists are fastened at one end to a ledger board attached to the house wall, and at the other end to a doubled band beam, which forms the perimeter of the porch. A doubled joist, installed at a 45° angle, gives extra support where the porch turns the corner, and short jack joists run between this corner joist and the band beam. The floor and its substructure are supported by traditional brick piers, which are in turn supported by concrete footings that extend below the frost line.

The carriages supporting a 9½-foot-wide set of steps are fastened at the top to the band beam and rest at the bottom on a shallow concrete footing. A fascia board is added to cover the rough lumber of the band beam, and lattice encloses the crawl space underneath the porch.

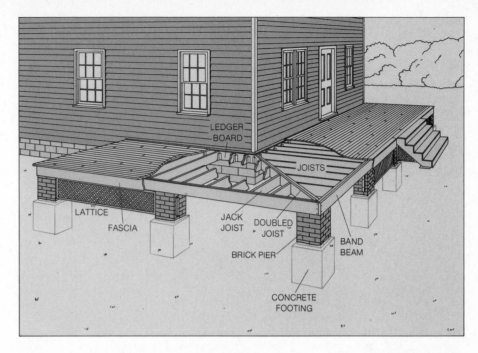

Plotting the Perimeter and Pouring Footings

1 **Squaring the corner.** Cut away siding to a height ¼ inch higher than the height of the proposed porch floor, taking care not to cut through the sheathing beneath; nail a 1-by-2 furring strip to each wall, ¼ inch below the top edge of the cut, to indicate the final porch height.

Using the strips for reference, set up triangulation for establishing the ends of the porch and its perimeter. First drive a nail into the top of one furring strip, 8 inches in from its outer end; add a second nail 6 feet from the first. Have a helper hook the end of a steel tape measure over each nail and pull both tapes away from the house. Where the 8-foot mark of the tape attached to the first nail intersects the 10-foot mark of the other tape, drive a 2-by-2 stake. Tie a string between the first nail and the stake.

Repeat this process at the other end of the furring strip to establish a straight line for the edge of the porch. Square off two identical lines in the same way on the second wing of the porch.

Cut two lengths of mason's cord, each 3 feet longer than the corresponding porch wing. Tie them to the outer stakes and stretch them along the inner stakes, toward the corner; where the cords intersect, drive a fifth stake to mark the point where the porch will turn a right angle. Set two more stakes beyond that point (inset), and tie the ends of the cords to them. Measure the distance from the corner stake to the corner of the house. The distance should be 11 feet 3¾ inches; if it is not, adjust the stake.

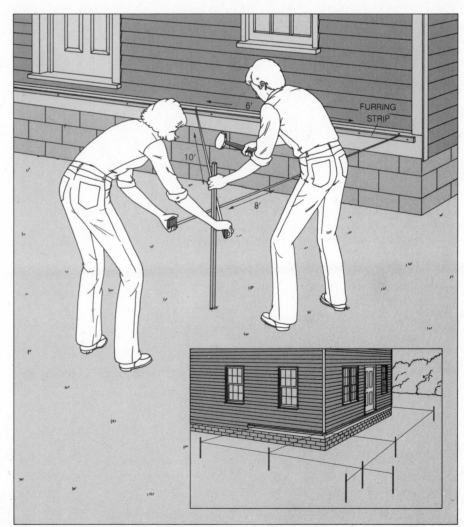

2 **Setting up batter boards.** Two feet out from the boundary lines at the corner at the end of each wing, erect two pairs of 2-by-4 stakes for two perpendicular batter boards. Using a water level and the top of the furring strip as a guide, mark the porch height on the stakes. Cut two 1-by-6 batter boards about 3 feet long. Hold one board against a pair of stakes, lining up one end with the stake farthest from the cor-

ner Set the top edge of the batter board at the final height of the pier, in this example 9 inches below the porch height. Level the batter board, and nail it to the stakes.

Secure the second batter board to the other pair of stakes, at a right angle to the first. Then set batter boards at the outer corner of the other wing and at the corner where the two wings

come together. To establish pier centers, mark the boundary line at regular intervals, beginning at the outer corners—in this example, at 9-feet-4-inch intervals. Tie a string marker at each pier center. Measure 1 foot to each side of each marker, and 2 feet out from the boundary line, to set stakes for a 1-by-6 batter board outside each pier location. Fasten the batter boards to the stakes at the final pier height.

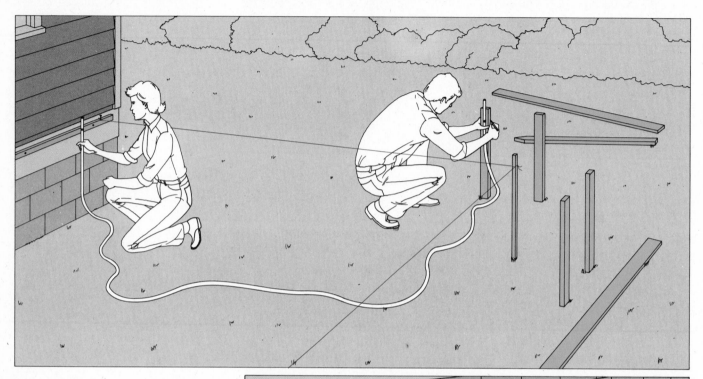

3 **Marking footing locations.** To mark the width of each footing, drop a plumb line at three points along the boundary line: one at the string marker indicating the pier center, the second and third from points 10 inches to either side of the pier center. Mark the ground with powdered chalk, and connect the marks with a chalk line. Parallel to this line, 2 inches out from the porch boundary, draw a second chalk line of the same length. At each end of this line, draw a perpendicular line extending 16 inches toward the house. Complete the 16-by-20-inch rectangle.

For the larger footing of the corner pier, use the corner stake as the marker for the outside corner of the pier; drop plumb lines 2 inches out from the stake's outside faces. Connect the marks with a chalk line, forming a right angle. Then, using a try square (a small framing square), extend the lines to construct a 20-inch square.

When all footing locations are outlined, set up a second set of boundary lines between nails driven partway into the tops of the corner batter boards. Remove the original boundary lines and stakes, and temporarily remove the new lines; leave the nails in the batter boards.

4 **Digging and pouring the footings.** Dig each footing hole to the required depth *(page 8)*. Start the excavation with a shovel, and remove the loosened dirt with a posthole digger. Tamp the soil at the bottom of each hole, to level it.

Pour concrete into each hole until the top is 3 inches below ground level. Slice through the wet concrete with a shovel, to remove air bubbles and to push large pebbles below the surface. Cover the footings with moist burlap and allow them to set for 24 to 48 hours.

5 **Marking footings for brick piers.** Retie the boundary lines to the nails in the batter boards *(opposite, Step 3)*, and add string markers to establish pier centers over the footings, every 9 feet 4 inches in this example. Drop a plumb line from each string marker, and mark where the plumb bob touches the footing. Drop the line again 8 inches to each side of the string marker, and connect the three marks. Use a try square to draw a 12-by-16 inch rectangle on each footing. For the large corner pier, use the same method to draw a 16-inch square.

Building Brick Piers

1 **Laying the first course.** Wearing gloves and using a pointed mason's trowel, spread a layer of mortar about ⅜ inch thick over the chalked rectangle on top of the footing. Then butter, or spread, adjoining brick surfaces with mortar, and lay the first course of bricks in the pattern shown here, butting ends to sides. If you are using bricks with one smooth side, be sure to lay each brick so that its kiln, or rough, side points toward the center. Trowel away excess mortar, and check the corners with a try square.

To lay the second course, spread a layer of mortar over the first course and, again buttering adjoining surfaces as you go along, lay the bricks in a staggered pattern, so that each joint in the first course is overlapped by a brick in the second course *(right, top inset)*. Continue in this way up the pier, alternating the brick patterns. At the end of each course, use a convex jointer to shape and smooth the joints.

For the larger corner pier, lay the first course in the pattern shown in the inset at bottom right. Stagger the bricks in each course as before, so that the previous joints are always covered.

2 **Completing the brick piers.** When you are halfway to the planned height of the pier, check your work by standing a mason's rule on the last course and, using a mason's level, sight to the pier-top mark on the batter board. If the distance between the mark and the last course does not divide into a whole number, adjust the thickness of the mortar on the last few courses at the top to compensate.

When all the piers are completed, fill their hollow centers with mortar and chipped brick. When the mortar has cured, mark the pier tops for the position of a doubled band beam. The inner edge of the beam will lie parallel to and 3 inches in from the outer face of every pier; scribe a line at this point. Remove the batter boards.

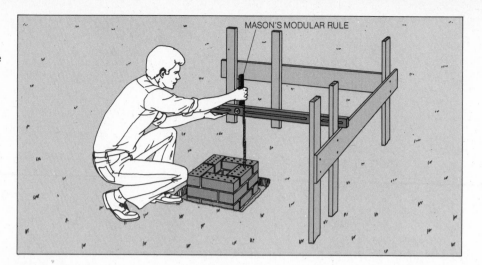

Matching Joist Size to Load and Span

	Lumber type and spacing			
Board size	No. 1 grade 16 in. o.c.	No. 1 grade 24 in. o.c.	No. 2 grade 16 in. o.c.	No. 2 grade 24 in. o.c.
2 × 6	9 ft. 9 in.	7 ft. 11 in.	8 ft. 7 in.	7 ft. 0 in.
2 × 8	12 ft. 10 in.	10 ft. 6 in.	11 ft. 4 in.	9 ft. 3 in.
2 × 10	16 ft. 5 in.	13 ft. 4 in.	14 ft. 6 in.	11 ft. 10 in.

Determining the dimensions of joists. This chart lists maximum spans for 2-by-6, 2-by-8 and 2-by-10 joists, assuming a load of 60 pounds per square foot. A porch or deck built for such a load is sturdy enough to enclose later on.

The recommended woods are those best for outdoor building—pressure-treated Douglas fir and southern pine. Joist spacing, 16 inches or 24 inches from center to center (commonly abbreviated as o.c.—on center), is determined by local codes. Either No. 1 or No. 2 lumber is appropriate for porches and decks; No. 1 lumber is stronger and looks better but is more expensive.

Building the Substructure

1 **Marking and installing ledger boards.** Draw a line along the house wall at the top of the furring strip, then remove the strip. Cut 2-by-8 ledger boards the length of the two porch wings, butt-joining them at the corner. Mark a bolt position on the board 4 inches from the outer end of each wing. Mark the succeeding bolt positions 16 inches apart, up to the porch corner.

Two inches above the center of the board, drill ¼-inch holes even with every other mark. Two inches below the board center, drill a second row of ¼-inch holes aligned with the remaining marks. Then tack the ledger against the house ¾ inch below the guideline, mark the hole positions on the house wall and remove the ledger. Along the upper row of hole positions, drill ¼-inch pilot holes in the wall. Along the bottom row, use a hammer drill (inset) to make ¾-inch holes, 4 inches deep, for the lag shields in the house foundation. Push expansion shields into the foundation holes; then replace the ledger, aligning all of the holes. Bolt the ledger to the house wall with ½-inch lag bolts, 4 inches long.

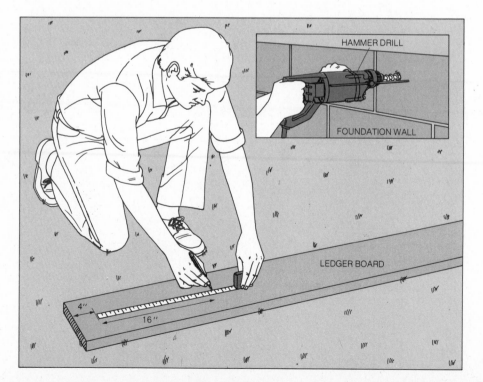

2 **Marking joist positions.** Starting at the outer end of each wing, use a framing square to mark joist positions on the ledger boards. Mark the first joist flush with the end of the ledger. Mark the subsequent joists on 16-inch centers, ending with the last joist before the corner.

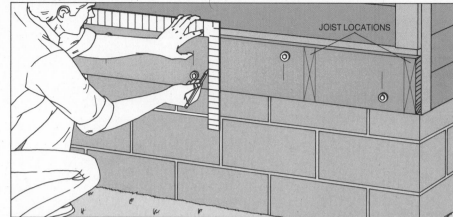

3 **Installing the first joists.** To mark the first joist for cutting, attach an L-shaped, all-purpose metal hanger to one end of a 2-by-8 and, while a helper holds that end against a joist mark on the ledger, mark where the other end of the 2-by-8 crosses the scribed line on the pier. Remove the joist and cut it.

Install all the joists that are to rest atop 12-by-16-inch piers. Resting one end of each joist on its pier, tap a U-shaped joist hanger onto the other end. Hold the joist against the ledger, top edges level, and nail the hanger to the ledger. Then nail the hanger to the joist.

4 **Installing the doubled band beam.** Starting at an outer corner, cut a 2-by-8 to span two adjacent piers; position one end flush with the outer face of the first joist, and trim off the other end about 3 inches beyond the joist resting on the adjacent pier. Nail the 2-by-8 to the two joists. Continue to add 2-by-8s between all the 12-by-16-inch piers, trimming them to end about 12 inches beyond the joists. Then measure, cut and install the remaining full-length joists between piers, attaching them to the ledger board with U-shaped joist hangers and face-nailing them to the 2-by-8s. Cut a second set of 2-by-8 band-beam boards to span adjacent piers, offsetting their joints from those of the first set; nail the two sets of boards together at 16-inch intervals, using three nails placed in a vertical row.

To complete the porch perimeter, install a doubled band beam between the last 12-by-16-inch pier on each wing and the large 16-by-16-inch corner pier. The ends and sides of the boards should meet at the corner in a herringbone pattern (inset). Reinforce this joint by driving three nails in each set of boards.

5 **Making a doubled corner joist.** Measure the diagonal distance between the ledger boards and the band beams at the corner where the two porch wings meet. Mark this distance, plus 1½ inches, on two 2-by-8s, then cut parallel 45° miters at the ends of each board. Set the boards face to face so that the miters form a point at one end, to fit against the band beam, and a V at the other end, to fit against the ledger. Nail the boards together from alternate sides at 16-inch intervals, positioning three nails vertically at each nailing point. Nail an adjustable L-shaped hanger to each side of the doubled joist at the end that joins the house (inset).

Position the doubled joist between the band beam and the ledger, bending the hangers to fit. Keeping the joist's top edge level with the top edges of the band beam and the ledger, nail the hangers to the ledger. Face-nail through the band beam into the other end of the joist.

6 **Installing the jack joists.** To support the wrap-around corner, nail jack joists between the diagonal doubled joist and the two band beams. Starting at the last full joist, mark the positions for the joist centers, 16 inches apart, on the band beams. At each mark set a board on edge across the doubled joist and the band beam, squaring it with a try square, and mark the board for cutting. Do not cut joists for any distance less than 16 inches.

Tap a U-shaped joist hanger onto the outer end of each jack joist. While a helper holds the joist in place, outer end perpendicular to the band beam, toenail the mitered end to the corner joist. Then nail the joist hanger to the beam and the joist.

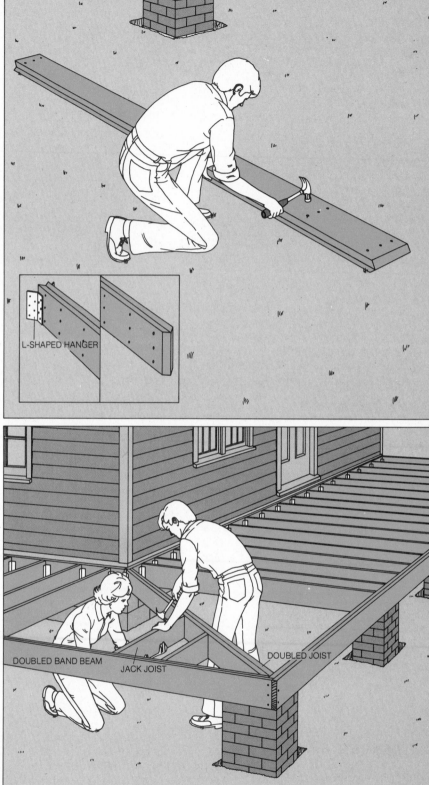

L-SHAPED HANGER

DOUBLED BAND BEAM
JACK JOIST
DOUBLED JOIST

Laying the Floorboards

1 Installing the outer rows of boards. Rip-cut the grooved edge from the first row of boards for one porch wing, and paint the cut edges with wood preservative. Starting where the two wings meet, nail the first row of boards to the band beam, tongued edges toward the house, with eightpenny (2½-inch) galvanized finishing nails every 16 inches. Position the boards so that their cut edges overhang the band beam by 1½ inches, and allow the two end boards to overhang the corners about 3 inches.

Trim the second row of boards so that their ends meet over joists, staggering the joints so that they do not line up with those in the preceding row. Before nailing the boards in place, measure their distance from the house wall at several points, to be sure they are parallel to it, and adjust the tongue-and-groove joint accordingly. Then drive eightpenny finishing nails through the tongue of each board into every joist. Install several more rows in this way.

MALLET

NAILER

DOUBLED JOIST

2 Using a power nailer. When you have installed enough floorboards to stand on, speed up the installation by using a power nailer for the remaining rows. Position a row of boards as in Step 1; then set the nailer head over the floorboard edge, and hit the spring-mounted mechanism with a mallet to drive a nail through the tongue into every joist. Continue installing boards, measuring the distance between the boards and the house every few rows to be sure they are still parallel. Do not install the last three rows against the house.

3 Mitering floorboards at the corner. Tack a 2-by-4 along the doubled corner joist, to serve as a guide for the base plate of a circular saw; position the guide so that the saw blade will lie directly over the seam of the doubled joist. Set the saw blade to the depth of the floorboards, and cut off all the boards on the first wing at once at a 45° angle. On the second wing—and on the last three rows of boards on both wings—trim each board individually to a 45° angle before installing it. If necessary, cut off the tongued edge of the very last row of

boards on both wings in order to fit the boards under the siding.

Nail through the face of each board into the joists below, using eightpenny nails; then caulk the seam at the house wall. At the outer end of each wing, snap a chalk line on the porch floor, perpendicular to the house wall and 1¾ inches out from the end joist. Trim the board ends along the line, leaving a 1¾-inch overhang. Sink exposed nail-heads, and fill the holes with wood putty.

Planning Stairway Dimensions

For appearance, the stairway descending from a large porch to the ground should be wide enough to span the distance between the centers of two foundation piers. Carriages—the notched boards that support the steps—are set no more than 30 inches apart; on a 9½-foot-wide staircase, such as the one described here, you will need four carriages. At the top of the stairway, the carriages are fastened to a back support, which fits against the band beam beneath the edge of the porch floor. At the bottom, the carriages rest on a concrete slab.

Before cutting the carriages, you must plan the stairway's dimensions. Start by measuring the total rise—the distance from the ground to the top surface of the porch floor. For the porch shown here, the total rise is 28 inches. Divide the total rise by 7 inches—the height of an average step—and round off the result to the nearest whole number, to determine the number of risers, or steps—in this example, four.

The unit run, or the depth of each step, should be at least 10 inches for an outdoor stairway. Make the stairway's total run, or the total horizontal distance from the porch to the front of the bottom step, the sum of the unit runs. For the four-step porch shown here, the total run is 40 inches, so the front of the bottom step should be 40 inches out from the porch.

Installing the Stairway

1 **Laying out the stairs.** Mark the total run of the stairway on a mason's level, using masking tape. Butt the end of the level against the band beam beneath the porch floorboards, and hold a folding ruler perpendicular to the level at the masking tape. Have a helper drive a small stake, to mark the point where the end of the ruler touches the ground. Mark two more points in the same way, along the width of the stairway. Connect the marks with a line the exact width of the stairway. Then chalk an outline for a trench 2 inches in front of the line, 12 inches behind it, and 6 inches beyond each end. Dig the trench 4 inches deep, and fill it with concrete to grade.

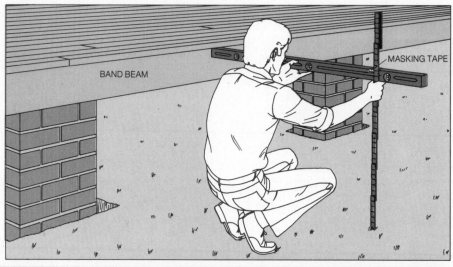

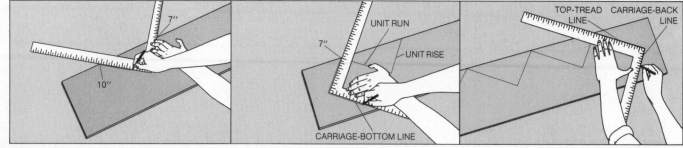

2 **Marking and cutting the carriages.** Set a framing square near one end of a 2-by-12 that has been cut 1 foot longer than the diagonal distance from the top of the band beam to the front edge of the concrete footing. Locate the unit-run number on one arm of the square, the unit-rise number on the other, and place the square on the 2-by-12 in such a way that both of the numbers (10 and 7, in the example here) are touching the upper edge of the board. Then mark the outline of the framing square's outer edges (*above, left*).

Turn the framing square clockwise until the unit-rise number— 7, in this example—touches the end of the previously drawn unit-run line. Again mark the outline of the square's outer edges, extending the carriage-bottom line all the way to the edge of the stock (*above, center*). Continue marking off pairs of perpendicular lines, one pair for each step—in this example, four pairs. Trace the last unit-run line—the line for the top tread—and continue around the framing square to the edge of the stock, to scribe the line for the back of the carriage. Cut along the unit-rise and unit-run lines and along the lines for the carriage back and carriage bottom. Then use this first carriage as a template to cut as many carriages as required—in this example, four carriages are called for.

3 **Attaching the stairs to the porch.** Cut a 2-by-8 back support to span the distance between the centers of two piers. Cut 1½ inches off each carriage back, to allow for the thickness of the back support. Nail the carriages to the support, evenly spaced, driving three 16-penny (3½-inch) nails through the support into the back of each carriage. Set the assembly in place, bottom on the concrete slab, back support against the band beam beneath the porch floor. While a helper steadies the assembly, drive 16-penny nails at 8-inch intervals in a zigzag pattern, through the back support into the band beam.

Lay a piece of tread stock on the carriage tops. If it does not lie flush with the floor of the porch, plane the carriages to fit.

4 **Installing risers and treads.** Cut from 1-by-10 lumber four risers 7 inches wide and the length of the stair, and fasten them to the carriages with tenpenny (3-inch) galvanized finishing nails. Then cut four treads from pre-nosed 1-by-12 stock, allowing a 1-inch overhang at the front of each step and a 1-inch overhang at each side. Nail the treads to the carriages, butting the lower treads against the risers. Rip the top tread to fit against the edge of the last porch floorboard.

Cut 1-by-10 fascia boards to cover the rough lumber of the band beams and end joists; at the corners, miter the ends of the fascia at 45° angles. Attach the fascia with three eightpenny (2½-inch) galvanized finishing nails driven in a vertical pattern at 16-inch intervals. Where the fascia meets the back support of the stairway, cover the seam with ogee molding (inset).

A Crisscrossed Lattice Enclosure

Anatomy of a lattice screen. The lacy screen that is traditionally used to fill the openings between porch piers is made of 1⅝-inch-wide lattice strips nailed in a crisscross pattern onto a 2-by-2 rectangular frame sized to fit the openings. A trim strip of the same lattice is used to cover the nailed ends. The screen is slipped under the edge of the fascia and fastened to it from the back with nails driven through the frame of 2-by-2s. At the sides, the frame rests against two furring strips, nailed to the piers. On the last screen installed, the frame is nailed to the fascia and the furring strips from the front, and the nail holes are covered with wood putty. Similar lattice screens—made in the same way but mounted on triangular frames—may also cover the openings at the sides of the stairway.

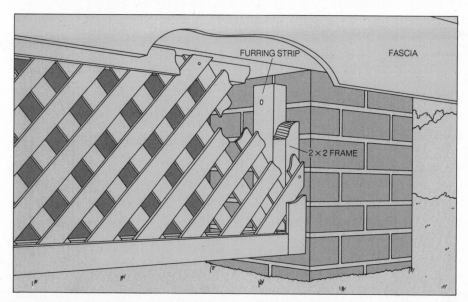

Wraparound Roof with an Angled Hip Rafter

No porch is complete without a covering. It may be as simple as a shed roof or as elaborate as the hip roof that covers the wraparound porch below. With its tongue-and-groove ceiling, enclosed ends and overhanging eaves, such a roof is a major undertaking. But if preliminary computations are carefully done, the parts will fit smoothly together.

The roof is supported at the house wall by two plates—one to hold the sloping rafters, the other to support the horizontal joists. For a typical ceiling, the joist plate is 8 feet above the porch floor, plus ½ inch to allow for ceiling boards. The distance between the plates is predicated on the desired pitch of the roof. Ideally,

the pitch should match that of the house roof, but since the rafter plate must be at least 3 inches below any second-story windows, adjustments may be necessary.

In constructing the roof, repeated use is made of a roofer's framing square, with a long arm called the body, and a short arm the tongue. The body is engraved with a reference table that is used to plot two sets of measurements. One set defines the diagonal ridge and tail cuts at the rafter ends and the bird's-mouth cut, which fits over the header. The other lets you calculate the lengths of the various rafters, as demonstrated at right.

Rafter lengths determine lumber sizes. In general, for rafters that span 8 feet

from the house to the header, you can use 2-by-6s; for spans up to 11 feet, 2-by-8s; for spans of more than 11 feet, 2-by-10s. Use joists, plates and headers of the same stock as the rafters. Porch posts are generally 4-by-4s; but if foundation piers are more than 9 feet apart, use 6-by-6s. To support 6-by-6 posts, nail braces—of the same stock as the band beam and as wide as each pier—to the inside of the band beam under the porch floor. The shingles on the porch roof should match those on the house. But you should substitute asphalt for tile or slate if the porch roof slopes less than 4 inches per foot, since both slate and tile need a slope steep enough to ensure fast water runoff.

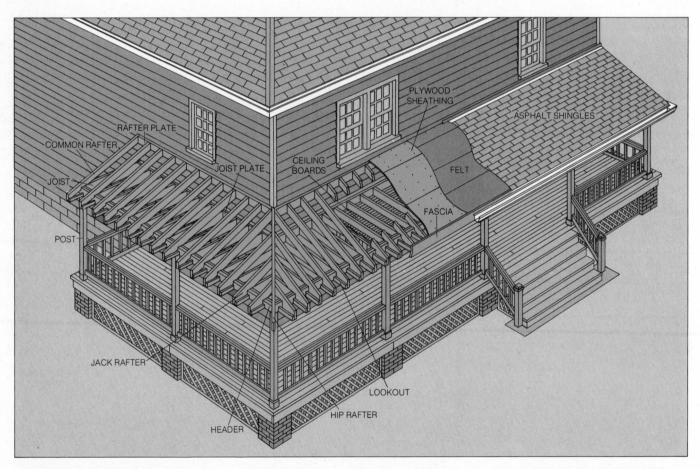

Anatomy of a wraparound porch roof. Horizontal joists and sloping common rafters spaced at 16-inch intervals form the skeleton of the porch roof. At the corner, a diagonal hip rafter and shorter jack rafters—and below them, jack joists—connect the two wings of the roof. The

joists and rafters are fastened at the house wall to joist and rafter plates; at the outer edge of the roof, where the joists and rafters meet, they are fastened to a doubled header—twin boards that sandwich a layer of plywood. The header is supported by posts centered over brick piers.

The porch roof is covered with ½-inch plywood sheathing, roofing felt, and asphalt shingles. Tongue-and-groove ceiling boards are nailed to the undersides of the joists. There are lookouts supporting the ceiling along the eaves and a fascia board trimming the edge.

Calculating Rafter Lengths

To calculate the length of a common rafter, first measure the rise and the run of the roof. The rise is the vertical distance from the top of the joist plate to the middle of the rafter plate. The run is the horizontal distance from the house wall to the outer edge of the header—which is located directly above the doubled band beam supporting the outer edge of the porch floor.

Using these figures, calculate the unit rise—the inches of rise per foot of run—by multiplying the rise by 12, then dividing the result by the run (in inches). For example, if—as in the diagram at right—the rise is 32 inches and the run is 8 feet (96 inches), multiply 32 by 12 and divide the result (384) by 96, yielding a unit rise of 4 inches per foot.

Now locate the unit rise on the body of the framing square, and read down from it to the number on the first line of the rafter table; this is the rafter length per foot of run. Multiply this reference number by the roof run, and divide the result by 12. With a unit rise of 4, for example, the reference number will be 12.65. Multiplied by the roof run, 8, then divided by 12, this reference number will yield a length of 8.43 feet—or 8 feet 5 inches. This is the length of a common rafter from the house wall to the header.

To determine the length of the overhang, draw a profile of the roof on graph paper, showing the actual dimensions of a rafter, a joist and the header—the same profile can also be used as a reference to the location of the ridge, bird's-mouth and tail cuts. Extend the rafter the desired distance of the overhang, and mark the position of the tail cut on the rafter's center line. (In this example, the overhang ends where the center line of the rafter intersects a horizontal line extended from the bottom of the header, ensuring that the ceiling of the porch and overhang will be continuous, as shown on page 28.)

Use the squares on the graph paper to measure the horizontal distance from the tail cut to the outer face of the header, in this example 24 inches. Multiply this number by the same reference number used to calculate the rafter length from house wall to header, 12.65; then divide by 12 to get the length of the overhang—in this case, 25.3 inches. Round off the overhang length and add it to the rafter length to get the total length for the common rafter.

Use the same calculation method (you will not need to make another drawing) but different reference numbers on the rafter table to determine the length of the hip rafter (*page 22, Step 1*) and the jack rafters (*page 24, Step 4*).

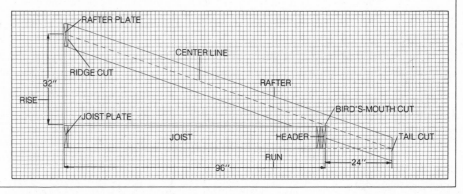

Erecting a Roof Support

1 **Snapping chalk lines for plates.** For each wing of the porch, snap two plumb chalk lines against the house wall—one 3 inches in from the outer end of the wing, the other at the corner of the house. Snap a horizontal chalk line 8 feet ½ inch above the porch floor to mark the bottom of the joist plate, then add a line to mark the top of the joist plate. Measure up from this line along the plumb lines to mark the bottom of the rafter plate; make this distance equal to the planned rise of the roof less half the width of the rafter plate. Then add a line to mark the top of the rafter plate, and connect the marks. Cut away siding where the joist plate and the rafter plate will lie, allowing extra space above the rafter plate to accommodate the thickness of your roofing materials. Cut joist and rafter plates; attach them to the wall studs, using staggered ⅜-inch-diameter lag bolts. If the joist plate lies against a plate in the wall, drive bolts in a straight line at 16-inch intervals. If you need more than one board for a porch wing, butt boards end to end. At the corner, overlap the board ends.

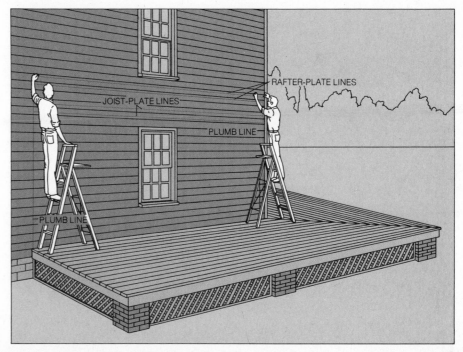

2 **Installing post anchors.** On each wing, snap a chalk line along the floor, directly above the outer face of the band beam. Mark the chalk lines 3 inches in from the outer end of each wing, and above the center of all the piers except the two end piers and the corner pier. Center a post anchor *(inset)* over each mark, its outer flange even with the chalk line; set the corner anchor at the intersection of the chalk lines. Place the offset washer inside the anchor, and mark the washer hole on the floor; then remove the anchor, and drill a ⅜-inch hole 5 inches deep through the floor into the band beam. Then fasten the anchor to the floor with a 5-inch-long ⅜-inch lag bolt. Set a post support in each anchor.

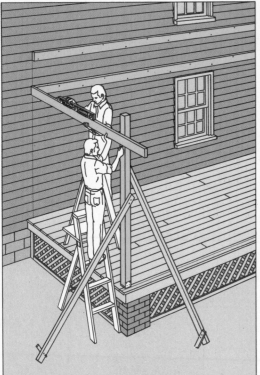

3 **Cutting and installing posts.** Set a post, slightly taller than the planned height of the porch ceiling, in the anchor at the end of one wing; brace it plumb with scrap 2-by-4s. Then tack one end of a joist to the end of the joist plate and, while a helper holds the board level, mark the position of its bottom edge on the post. Take down the post and the joist. Similarly, mark a post for the outer end of the other porch wing, then cut and compare the two posts. If they are the same length, cut all of the posts to that length. If they are different lengths, measure and cut each remaining post separately. Nail a post cap to the top of each post except the one at the corner, then set each post in its anchor and drive nails partway through the anchor and into the wood. Brace the posts plumb with 2-by-4s.

4 **Cutting and installing headers.** Cut a pair of boards to fit between the outside edge of an end post and the middle of the adjacent post. Sandwich a piece of ½-inch plywood, cut to the same length and width, between the two boards, and nail the assembly together from both sides with 12-penny (3¼-inch) nails spaced 10 inches apart and staggered. Assemble headers to fit across adjacent pairs of posts, cutting the boards so that their ends meet over post tops. Then set the headers atop the posts, and nail them to the post caps; toenail the abutting ends of adjacent headers together. Stop at the last post before the corner, then install headers on the other wing.

At the corner post, miter the ends of the headers at a 45° angle *(inset)*; nail the ends to each other and toenail the headers to the post.

5 **Squaring the frame.** Remove the 2-by-4 braces from an end post and replace them with a horizontal 2-by-4, tacked to the ends of the joist plate and the header. To square the corner formed by the brace and the header, set a framing square inside it and tap both boards with a hammer until they fit snugly against the square. Add a second, diagonal 2-by-4 brace across the tops of the header and joist plate, as indicated by the dotted lines. Then add a third 2-by-4 brace, parallel to the first, at the mid-point of the wing. Brace the other wing in the same way. After the roof frame is squared, finish nailing the posts to the anchors. Beginning 2 inches from the house corner and working out toward the end of each wing, install ceiling joists spaced 16 inches on center, attaching them with joist hangers. Remove the diagonal and mid-point braces as you approach them. Toenail the end joist to the plate and the header instead of using hangers. Install corner joists and jack joists as for a floor *(page 14, Steps 5 and 6)*. When all joists are installed, remove the braces.

Cutting and Installing Common Rafters

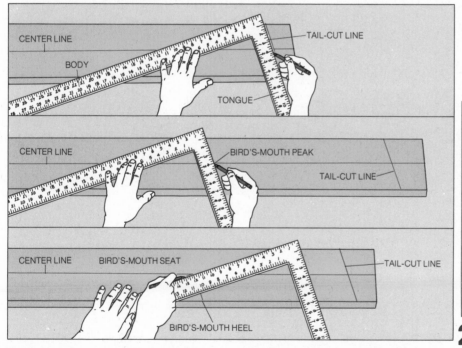

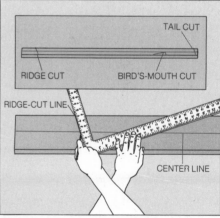

1 **Laying out a tail cut and a bird's-mouth cut.** Snap a chalk line lengthwise along the center of the rafter. Set the framing square across the outer end of the board so that the number 12 on the outer edge of the body, and the unit-rise number on the outer edge of the tongue, line up with the chalk line. (The 12 is a constant for all common rafters; the 4 is the unit rise for this particular roof.) Draw a line along the outer edge of the tongue to mark the tail cut. To mark the bird's-mouth cut, measure along the center line from the tail cut, and mark off the length

of the overhang; this mark establishes the peak of the bird's-mouth. Set the unit-rise number at the peak and the 12 on the center line, as before, and draw a line along the outer edge of the tongue from the peak to the bottom edge of the rafter; this establishes the heel of the bird's-mouth *(above, center)*. Then slide the square down the rafter, setting the 12 on the peak and the unit-rise number on the center line; draw a line along the outer edge of the body from the peak to the rafter's bottom edge, to establish the seat of the bird's-mouth *(above, bottom)*.

2 **Marking a ridge cut.** To mark the ridge cut—where the top end of the rafter will butt against the rafter plate—start at the bird's-mouth peak and measure along the center line the length of the rafter minus 1½ inches—the thickness of the rafter plate. Mark this point on the center line. Then reverse the framing square; line up the unit-rise number on the outer edge of the tongue with the mark, and the 12 on the outer edge of the body with the center line. Draw a line along the outer edge of the tongue. Make the ridge cut and the tail cut with a circular saw. Use a saber saw or a handsaw to make the bird's-mouth cut.

3 **Testing the rafter for fit.** Tack a rafter hanger flush with the outer end of the rafter plate. With a helper, set the rafter in position; the ridge cut should be against the hanger, the bird's-mouth resting on the header. Tack the rafter to the hanger, then check the fit of the cuts at both ends. The ridge cut should butt tightly against its hanger, and the bird's-mouth should fit snugly around the header. If any of the cuts are off by more than ⅛ inch, recut the rafter. When the rafter fits properly, mark it and use it as a template to cut all of the remaining common rafters (*inset*), one for each full-length joist.

4 **Installing the common rafters.** Nail L-shaped, all-purpose metal hangers (*page 13*) to the rafter plates, using a plumb bob to center one over each joist except the one nearest the corner of the house. For that joist, toenail a rafter flush with the corner formed by the rafter plates, and set its bird's-mouth over the header. Attach a special wing-shaped rafter anchor to the header at the point where the rafter and the header meet; it will be slightly to the side of the nearest joist (*inset*). Nail the rest of the rafter anchors to the headers at the remaining joists.

Attach each rafter to the plate and the header, nailing through the anchor and the hanger into the rafter face. Then install the rafters along the other wing in the same manner.

Adding Hip and Jack Rafters

1 **Laying out the hip rafter.** Find the length of the hip rafter and its overhang as for a common rafter (*page 19*), but use the reference number on the second line of the rafter table on the framing square. Then snap a chalk line down the center of each face of the rafter. Mark tail and bird's-mouth cuts on the rafter (*page 21, Step 1*), using the number 17 on the body of the square as the constant instead of the number 12. Locate the ridge cut by measuring along the center line the rafter length minus 2¼ inches— the thickness of the diagonal corner joint of the rafter plates. Mark the ridge cut as for a common rafter (*page 21, Step 2*), again using the number 17 as the constant. Mark the opposite face of the rafter with identical ridge-cut and tail-cut lines. Connect each pair of lines with a squared line across the top edge of the rafter, then mark the midpoint of each squared line.

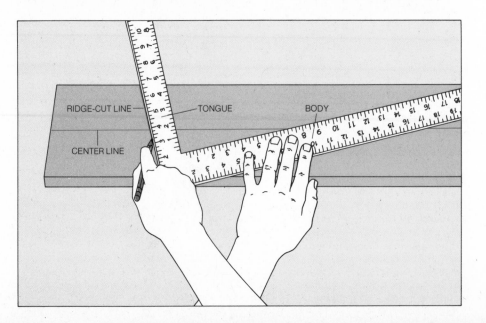

RIDGE-CUT LINE — TONGUE — BODY

CENTER LINE

2 **Marking the bevel cuts.** To find the angle for the side of the compound ridge cut, read down from the unit-rise number to the sixth line on the body of the framing square. Set the rafter on edge and place the square, its angle toward you, so that the outer edge of the body crosses the midpoint of the squared line that connects the ridge-cut lines. Set the number 12, on the outer edge of the body, against the edge of the rafter (top right). Set the side-cut number—in this example 11$\frac{11}{16}$—on the outer edge of the tongue against the same edge of the rafter. Draw a line from the center mark down the outer edge of the body. Then reverse the square so that the angle points away; position it as before and mark a second line, forming a V. Extend the V along both faces of the rafter, parallel to the ridge-cut lines. Measure the angle between the squared line and the side lines, using a T bevel. Set the blade of a circular saw to that angle, and cut both faces of the board along the lines marking the side cuts (inset, top).

To mark side cuts at the tail, position the square as for the ridge cuts, but draw the first line up the body; then reverse the square for the second line (bottom right). Extend and cut the lines as for the ridge cut, to make the tail side cuts (inset, bottom). Then cut the bird's-mouth.

3 **Beveling the rafter top.** Draw a center line along the top of the rafter, to mark the top of the bevel. Then, to determine the angle of the bevel cut, first bisect the line near the middle of the rafter. Position the framing square, its angle away from you, so that the unit-rise number on the outer edge of the tongue touches the top edge of the rafter. Using the figure on the second line of the rafter table as the reference number, swing the square until this number on the body of the square touches the top edge of the rafter. Then slide the square until the outer edge of the tongue passes through the center point, and draw a line along the outer edge of the tongue (right, top). Measure the distance between the top end of this line and the squared line—in this example the two lines are $\frac{3}{16}$ inch apart. Mark this distance from the top at several points along the rafter faces. Connect the marks to make guidelines (indicated by the dashed line), and with a jack plane bevel between both guidelines and the center line (bottom right). Raise the hip rafter, fitting the ridge cut into the angle formed by the two common rafters at the house corner and resting the bird's-mouth over the corner formed by the headers. Nail through the common rafters into the hip rafter; toenail the bottom to the headers.

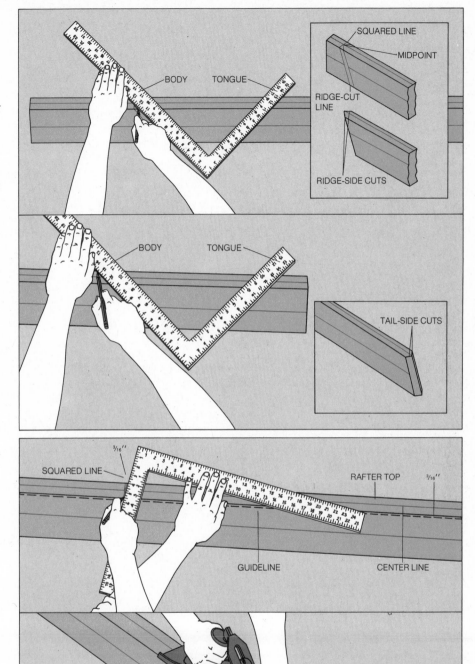

SQUARED LINE

MIDPOINT

RIDGE-CUT LINE

RIDGE-SIDE CUTS

BODY   TONGUE

BODY   TONGUE

TAIL-SIDE CUTS

SQUARED LINE $\frac{3}{16}$''

RAFTER TOP $\frac{3}{16}$''

GUIDELINE   CENTER LINE

CENTER LINE

GUIDELINE

4 **Cutting the first jack rafter.** Find the length of the first (shortest) jack rafter under the unit-rise number on the third line of the rafter table. Snap a chalk line along the center of a board that is slightly longer than this length plus the overhang. Mark the tail and bird's-mouth cuts (*page 21, Step 1*), using 12 as the constant. To locate the ridge cut, measure from the bird's-mouth peak along the center line the length of the rafter minus 1⅛ inches—half the diagonal thickness of the hip rafter. Lay out a ridge cut as on page 21, Step 2. Square a line across the top of the rafter from the ridge-cut line (*page 22, Step 1*), and

mark its midpoint. Find the reference number for the ridge cut's bevel on the fifth line on the rafter table under the unit-rise number. Set the square on the rafter top as shown, aligning the 12 on the outer edge of the body with the midpoint of the squared line, the bevel number on the outer edge of the tongue with the rafter's top edge (*below*). Draw a line along the outer edge of the body; extend it down the rafter face, parallel to the ridge-cut line (*inset*). Measure the angle between the squared line and the bevel line; set a circular saw to that angle and cut along the bevel line. Then cut the tail and bird's-mouth cuts.

5 **Installing the jack rafters.** Cut the remaining jack rafters for one side of the hip rafter, using the same method as in Step 4, increasing the length of each successive rafter by the number under the unit rise on the third line of the rafter table. Fasten the jack rafters to the hip rafter with L-shaped, all-purpose metal hangers and to the header with rafter anchors.

Cut jack rafters for the other side of the hip, using the same method; but in marking the bevel, point the angle of the square toward you so that you are using the bevel number on the body and the 12 on the tongue.

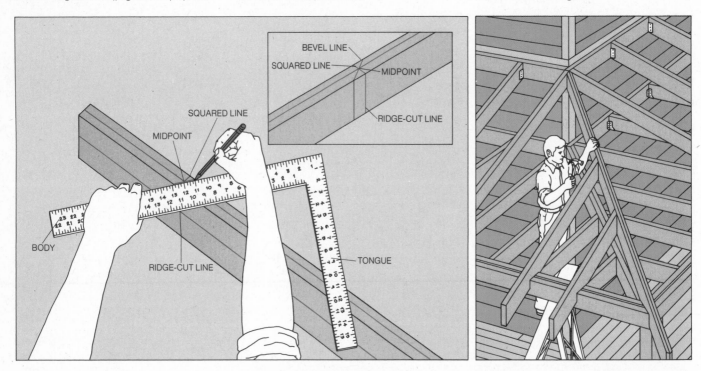

Preparing for Shingles

1 **Installing the plywood sheathing.** Starting at the outer end of a porch wing, fasten sheets of Type C-D plywood horizontally, C side up, along the eave, overlapping the rafter tails by ¾ inch and the end rafter by 3 inches. Leave ¹/₁₆ inch (⅛ inch in very humid climates) between adjacent sheets of plywood. Butt-join the ends of sheets over a rafter, nailing each sheet to the rafter at 6-inch intervals; along intermediate rafters, drive nails at 1-foot intervals. When you reach the hip rafter, cut the end of the plywood sheet at an angle, so that it lines up with the midpoint of the rafter. Continue to nail additional rows of plywood up the roof, staggering the joints between sheets. Nail temporary 2-by-4s to the plywood as you go along, for footholds. Cut the last row of plywood sheets so that they will fit snugly against the house sheathing just below the edge of the siding.

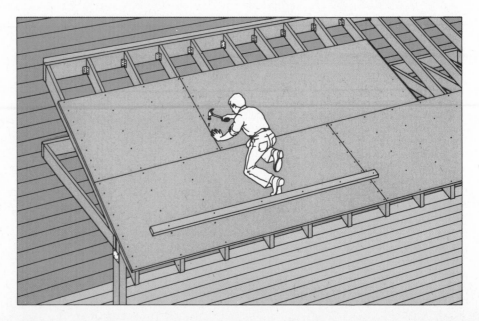

2 **Adding the roofing felt.** Leaving a 6-inch overhang at the outer end of one wing, unroll a strip of
15-pound roofing felt along the eave, extending it at least 1 foot beyond the hip rafter. Tack
the felt to the plywood sheathing, using roofing nails driven partway in at 3-foot intervals,
8 inches from the top and bottom edges of the
strip. Tack the outer end with two nails, 6 inches
in from the edge of the plywood. Smooth the
felt flat, moving the nails if necessary. Then drive
all of the nails into the plywood, but do not allow the heads to break through the felt. Trim the
felt flush with the plywood at the outer end of
the wing. Fold the felt at the corner over the hip,
and nail it to the plywood on the other wing.
Trim the felt to extend 1 foot beyond the hip.

Working up the roof, nail on additional strips of
felt, overlapping the strips 2 inches. If a roll ends
in mid-roof, overlap the new strip 4 inches and
fasten the seam with nails every 6 inches. Complete the second wing in the same way. Cover
the eave line of the roof with an aluminum drip
edge, flush with the edge of the plywood (inset). Drive roofing nails at 1-foot intervals through
the center of the drip edge.

DRIP EDGE

Laying Shingles

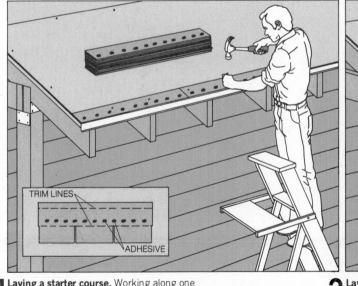

TRIM LINES

ADHESIVE

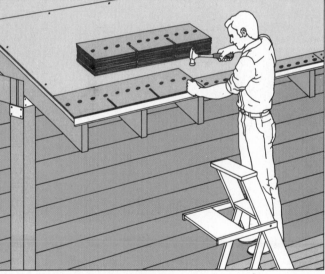

1 **Laying a starter course.** Working along one
wing, from the outer end to the hip, lay a row of
starter strips end to end, bottom edge of the
strips overlapping the top of the drip edge. Fasten
each strip to the roof with three roofing nails,
spaced evenly along the center. To form each
starter strip, trim down standard 1-by-3-foot
asphalt roofing; cut 2 inches from the top,
5 inches from the bottom, leaving a strip 3 feet
long and 5 inches wide (inset). Trim 6 inches from
the end of the first starter strip so that the
joints in the first course of shingles will not line
up with the joints between the starter strips. Trim
the last strip even with the crest of the hip rafter.

2 **Laying the first course.** Lay the first row of
shingles directly over the starter course. Fasten
each shingle strip with four 1¼-inch roofing
nails placed in a row ⅝ inch above the slots that
divide the strip into tabs. Place a nail above
each slot, a nail 1 inch in from each end. Trim the
last strip even with the crest of the hip rafter.

Measure the depth of the exposed shingles on
the main house roof, then divide the porch roof
into rows of the same depth. If the result yields
a last row of exposed shingles narrower than
4 inches, adjust the depth of the last four to six
rows to keep the last row from being too narrow.

3 **Working up the roof.** Cut 6 inches, or half of a tab, from the end of the first shingle strip in the second row. Align the cut end with the end of the first shingle in the first course, overlapping it to leave an exposed edge, as calculated in Step 2. If the last shingle tab at the hip will be shorter than 6 inches, cut off half the end tab from the preceding strip and add 6 inches to the shingle at the hip.

Continue to lay successive courses, each time trimming the first shingle 6 inches shorter than the shingle in the preceding course. By the sixth course the first shingle section will be reduced to half a tab; start the seventh course with a full shingle. Adjust the exposure on the last few courses, if necessary, and butt the top edge of the last course of shingles against the house. Shingle the other wing in the same way.

4 **Adding hip shingles and roof flashing.** Cover the crest of the hip with individual shingle tabs, each creased along the center to fit over the crest. Set one shingle at the eave line, a second at the house wall and, with the aid of a helper, snap chalk lines down both sides of the hip to mark the edges of the hip shingles. Beginning at the eave and working up the hip, fasten each folded shingle tab to the hip with two nails, 2 inches above the adhesive strip, 1 inch in from the edge, matching the exposure of the hip shingles to those on the body of the roof. At the house wall, trim the top edge of the last shingle to fit against the wall corner of the house.

Install 8-inch-wide aluminum flashing between the house wall and the roof along each wing. Slip one edge of the flashing under the siding; bend the other edge to lap over the top row of shingles. At the hip, cut the flashing flush with the house corner. Use roofing cement to seal the seam where the two pieces of flashing meet and to attach the flashing to the shingles. Then nail it to the siding at 1-foot intervals (inset).

Side Enclosures and Soffit Supports

1 Installing lookouts. Use a level to mark the tail of each rafter flush with the bottom edge of the header, then cut off the rafter along the line. Cut 2-by-4s to fit between the header and each rafter tail; these pieces are called lookouts. Set the lower edge of the lookout flush with the bottom of the header and the newly cut edge of the rafter tail; toenail the lookout to the header, and face-nail it to the rafter (*inset, top*). Cut two lookouts for the hip rafter (*inset, bottom*), one for each side, mitering one end to fit flush against the header and the other to match the side cut on the hip rafter.

2 Enclosing the ends of the roof. Cut a piece of ½-inch exterior-grade plywood to cover the triangular space created by the rafter and the joist at the end of each wing. Extend the plywood ½ inch below the bottom of the joist, to cover the edge of the ceiling (*page 28*). Nail the plywood cover to the rafter and the joist. Then cut a rake board to match the length of the common rafters, but add 1½ inches so that the rake will overlap the end of the rafter plate. Butt the rake against the underside of the plywood sheathing, and nail it to the plywood cover. If the plywood sheathing on the roof extends past the outer face of the rake, trim the angle with a strip of quarter-round molding.

3 Adding a fascia and gutters. Cut lengths of 1-inch-thick fascia board to cover the rafter tails, making the fascia about 2 inches wider than the depth of the tails. Slip the fascia up into the space between the tails and the drip edge, lining up the outer end of the fascia with the outer face of the rake board and butt-joining fascia boards over rafter tails. Nail the fascia to the rafter tails. At the corner where the two wings meet, miter the ends of the fascia at a 45° angle.

Using the fasteners supplied by the manufacturer, attach gutters to the fascia and downspouts to the corner post and end posts (*inset*). Seal all the gutter joints with waterproof mastic.

27

A Ceiling and a Porch Railing

A ceiling and a railing are the finishing touches to the construction of a porch. Both are made of specially milled lumber, called porch stock, which is available from lumber suppliers.

Porch stock for ceilings consists of tongue-and-groove boards ½ inch thick and 3 inches wide with a bead down the center. They are generally installed from the house wall to the eave, forming one continuous surface (right, top). The boards can, however, end at the header, leaving the overhang to be enclosed by sheets of plywood called soffit boards.

To allow air to circulate within the small, enclosed area of the overhang, screen vents are installed in the ceiling boards or in the soffit. The vents are available in several shapes and sizes at hardware stores; your local building code will specify the correct size and spacing for your area.

Porch stock for railings consists of cap rails, bottom rails and 1-by-1 pickets that fit vertically between the rails. Cap-rail stock is milled with a one-inch-wide groove on the underside, and bottom-rail stock comes with one angled face; this design allows easy installation of the pickets, which slip up into the groove of the cap rail and fit against the angled face of the bottom rail with a minimum of last-minute trimming and planing.

All three elements can be specially milled for specific decorative effects; but they also come in the standard stock shown here, available in 16-foot lengths that can be cut to fit any porch.

A tongue-and-groove porch ceiling. Tongue-and-groove boards are face-nailed to ceiling joists with sixpenny (2-inch) finishing nails; the nails are then set and the nail holes filled with putty. Installation begins at the house wall and ends at the fascia board, where a quarter-round molding covers the joint between the last ceiling board and the fascia. At the outer end of each porch wing, the boards butt against the inner face of the plywood triangle that encloses the side of the roof, and quarter-round molding, nailed to the plywood, covers the cut ends. Where the wings meet, the boards are mitered at a 45° angle.

The ceiling boards are notched to fit around the porch posts. Along the center of the overhang, holes are cut in the boards to make space for vent screens (inset) to be installed.

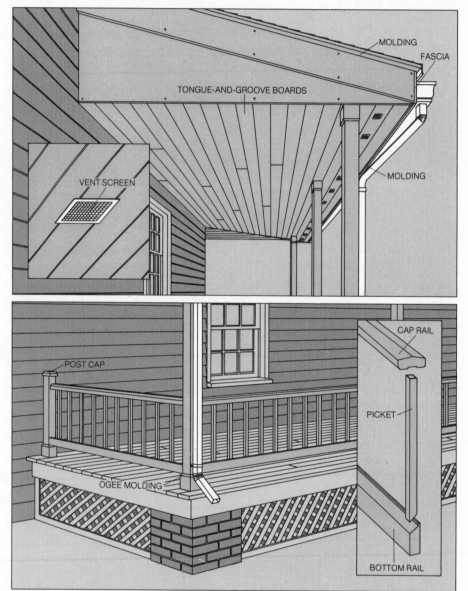

A railing to surround the porch. The support posts for the railing are 4-by-4s, cut 2 inches longer than the height of the railing and installed on post anchors, in line with the full-length porch posts. One post is placed against the house wall at the end of each wing; others are installed wherever two full-length porch posts are more than 8 feet apart. The bottom of each post is encased with 1-by-4 lumber topped by ½-inch ogee molding. Angled bottom rails (inset) are toenailed to the posts above the molding, the angled face toward the house. Cap rails are toenailed to the posts 30 to 40 inches above the floor, or as specified by local codes.

Pickets are of 1-by-1 stock and toenailed 8 inches apart—or at the intervals specified by local codes—to the cap and bottom rails. The lower end is cut to match the angle of the bottom rail, and the top of the picket fits into the 1-inch groove on the underside of the cap rail. Simple post caps are toenailed to the tops of the posts.

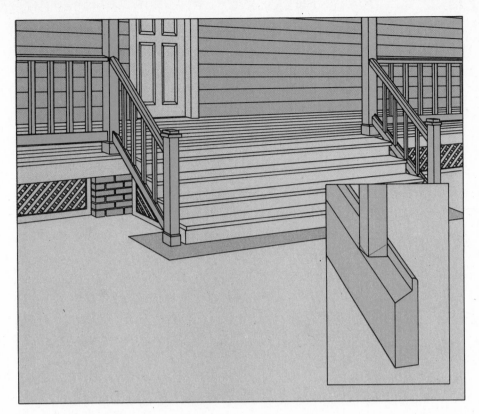

A railing for the porch stairs. Posts for the bottom of the stairs, cut to the same height as the other railing posts *(opposite, bottom)*, are fastened with post anchors to the concrete footing directly against both sides of the bottom step. The anchor's flanges are covered with trim, as on the porch posts.

Bottom rails and cap rails are mitered to fit snugly between the full-length porch posts, at the top of the stairs, and the bottom posts. Pickets are similarly mitered to match the slope of the cap rail; their bottom ends are cut to fit the angled face of the bottom rail, then mitered to match the slope of the bottom rail *(inset)*. The stair pickets are spaced and toenailed in the same way as those on the porch *(opposite, bottom)*.

Classical Columns for Purists

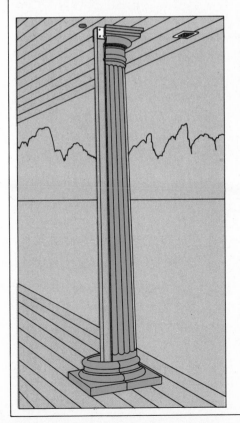

Instead of square porch posts, you may prefer to use cylindrical columns, long associated with the traditional American porch. You can order them, plain or fluted, with Ionic, Doric or Corinthian capitals, from most large lumberyards, in lengths from 8 to 20 feet.

The columns may be solid, supporting the roof in lieu of posts, or they may be hollow, to fit around posts like a sleeve. Solid columns are generally less than 5 inches in diameter and are made by turning a wooden beam on a lathe. Hollow columns are made of aluminum or are constructed from long strips of wood that are held together down the length of the shaft by tongue-and-groove joints and glue.

The base and the capital of an aluminum column are commonly molded in one with the shaft. On a hollow wooden column, the base and the capital usually are separate elements; sometimes they are additionally subdivided into horizontal sections.

Columns may be installed, like posts, in the course of framing the roof; or, if the roof is temporarily supported by 4-by-4s during construction, the columns can be slipped in afterward. Hollow columns that are separated into two vertical sections are fitted around the porch posts after the roof is built.

Before connecting these parts, protect the inside of the column from moisture by coating the bottom with roofing compound to a height of 2 feet and ventilating the top with two holes in the ceiling or soffit. One hole should be inside the column, the other within a foot of the exterior. If the capital protrudes past the fascia, the column must also be protected from rain by a strip of aluminum flashing, nailed to the ceiling or the soffit so that the top of the capital is covered.

To install the parts of a hollow wooden column, first join half the capital to half the shaft. Attach the base pieces to the porch floor around the post; then attach the assembled half column to the base. Add the other section of shaft and capital, and finally attach the assembled capital to the ceiling.

Decks That Blend into Their Surroundings

A deck is a crossbreed, combining some of the best features of both porches and patios. Like the old-fashioned porch, it is made of wood and sits aboveground. But it also has the open, airy feeling of a patio, serving as an architectural transition zone between indoors and out.

There are almost as many ways to build a deck as to build a house. The method shown on these pages exploits a deck's most desirable qualities. Because the number of support posts is kept to a minimum, the structure seems to float in space and to be part of both the house and the landscape.

Built in this way, a deck can hug the ground or ride high above it. And the basic design can be modified or embellished for a variety of situations. Differing railing and decking treatments can be used. Multiple levels can be achieved with separate structures, linked by stairways to allow passage from one level to another. Sliding glass doors *(pages 120-127)*, installed just before the railings, provide easy access from the house to a second-story deck. Built-in seating *(page 128)* and trellis-like shade roofs *(page 108)* are other possible variations.

Deck building has been simplified by the availability of lumber that has been pressure-treated with wood preservative to resist rot. But pressure-treated wood often has a green tinge that takes up to a year to bleach to gray. Alternatively, you can use redwood or cedar for the decking and railing. Both are rot-resistant and have pleasant color and texture. Unfinished redwood and cedar will also eventually turn gray—redwood, dark gray.

Plan your deck on paper by first making a scale drawing of the side of the house to which it will be attached. Establish positions for the basic structural elements: the ledger board to be attached to the house wall, the two joists that run perpendicular to the house at the ends of the ledger, and the ribbon board, which defines the outer edge of the deck. Then decide where you want the supporting posts and add a beam, paralleling the ledger, right over the posts. The posts should be no more than 8 feet apart, and the beam should overhang the posts by no more than 2 feet on each side.

In plotting the post locations, beware of buried telephone cables and underground lines for gas, water and electricity; utility companies can tell you where they are. Keep in mind, too, that the beam should fall somewhere in the last quarter of the distance between the ledger and the ribbon board.

The span between the beam and the ledger dictates joist size and spacing. (For the relationship between span and joist size, see page 12.) If you change the position of the posts and the beam slightly, you may be able to use a smaller size of lumber not only for the joists but for the beam, which is the same lumber doubled, and for the ledger and ribbon boards, also of joist-size lumber.

When you have plotted the basic structure, add to your deck plan any other features you wish to incorporate. Then make a list of materials needed. When you buy the lumber, get an extra board or two in each size and, if possible, get decking boards in lengths just slightly longer than you need. Also, look for straight decking boards, to eliminate the tricky carpentry *(page 35)* needed to correct warped boards. When you get to the lumberyard, you may find that a modest alteration in your plan will let you buy stock lumber sizes and reduce waste.

In assembling the deck you will need lag bolts for joining the ledger to the house wall, ½-inch carriage bolts for attaching the railings and posts, and 12-penny (3¼-inch) spiral-shanked electroplated nails—or, if you use redwood, acid-resistant aluminum nails—to attach the decking and railings. The joists are suspended from joist hangers and metal angle reinforcements. Supporting posts and beams are joined with metal post-and-beam ties and joists are fastened to the beam with metal brackets called tie-downs. Allow four 60-pound bags of concrete for the footing of each post.

A subdivided deck. This deck in two parts, serving two rooms of a house, consists of a pair of platforms with a stairway between them. The platforms are anchored to the house by a single ledger and are supported at the other end by two beams, each resting on two 4-by-4 posts. The platform joists rest on the beams and extend beyond them, just as the outside ends of the beams project beyond the posts. The posts are anchored in concrete footings. Railings, omitted from the front platform here for clarity, are made of 4-by-4 posts with 2-by-6 rails and handrail. The 2-by-6 decking is laid in both straight and herringbone patterns.

Building the Basic Deck

1 Starting the platform. Put up a ledger 3 inches shorter than the planned width of the platform. Mark joist positions on it, following the techniques in Step 2, page 13. Then triple-nail a side joist, 1½ inches shorter than the planned depth of the deck, to one end of the ledger while a helper holds up the far end of the joist and keeps it level. Nail a temporary support to the far end of the joist, toenailing this support to a scrap of wood at ground level. Attach a second side joist to the opposite end of the ledger in the same way. Choose sound, straight boards for these two joists.

If the ledger is attached to lapped clapboard siding and does not rest on the crowns of two strips of clapboard, trim the ends of the side joists, and all intermediate joists, so that they will fit the siding angle snugly.

2 Adding a ribbon board. Cut a ribbon board to the planned width of the deck, and mark joist positions on it corresponding to those on the ledger. Triple-nail the ribbon board to the ends of the joists, to complete the basic frame of the platform. Shift the position of the frame slightly, if necessary, to square its corners. Cut two more joists to fit between the ledger and the ribbon board and attach them as in Step 3, page 13.

If you are building a deck close to the ground, so that using a posthole digger beneath the frame would be difficult, locate and dig the postholes (*Steps 6 and 7*) before constructing the frame.

RIBBON BOARD

3 **Stabilizing the frame.** While a helper holds a steel square against an outside corner of the frame, check the position of the ribbon board again, shifting it sideways until the corner of the frame nests exactly into the square. Then nail a long diagonal brace across the tops of the ribbon board, one or both intermediate joists and a side joist. Give the corner a final check to be sure the frame is absolutely square. Then hang the remaining joists with joist hangers nailed to the ledger and ribbon boards. Add metal angle reinforcements to the inside corners where the end joists meet the ledger and the ribbon board.

4 **Marking the beam position.** Measure out from the ledger along each side joist to the point where you want the inside face of the support beam to fall. Mark these points, then snap a chalk line across the underside of the joists between the marks. Nail metal tie-down brackets to the joists along the chalk line.

5 **Hanging the beam.** Cut two beam boards the width of the deck, and have a helper hold the first beam board in place while you are driving nails through the tie-downs into the board. Nail the second beam board against the outside face of the first one. If the beam is at head height or if you want to improve its appearance, cut off the lower corners of the beams at a 45° angle before installing them. If the deck is too wide for the available lumber, use two boards for each section, but offset the joints so that the boards meet at different points on the two sections.

6 **Locating the footings.** Mark the post positions along the beam. Use a plumb bob to find the corresponding points on the ground, and mark these points with stakes. If you are building a low deck, mark the post positions by squaring up the frame as in Step 3, marking the beam position on the side joists as in Step 4, and stretching a string between the marks. Locate the post positions on this string, and drop a plumb bob to find the corresponding positions on the ground.

7 **Digging the footing holes.** With a posthole digger, open a footing hole at each stake; make the holes at least 24 inches deep and 8 inches below the local frost line. Make the bottom diameter of the holes for the outer posts at least 12 inches across, those for the intermediate posts 16 inches across. The upper portion of each hole can be narrower than the bottom.

8 Hanging the supporting posts. Use a plumb line to mark post locations on the beam directly over the footing holes, and use post-and-beam ties to hang the 4-by-4 posts from the beam. Cut each post to reach from the beam to a point in the footing hole at or just above the frost line. Coat the cut ends liberally with a commercial wood preservative; a good way to do this is to set the posts in containers of preservative and let them soak. Nail the post-and-beam ties to the posts, then hold the posts against the beam and nail through the flange holes into the beam. For a tight fit, shim the back flange at each post with a ½-inch spacer. The posts should hang plumb but, if necessary, add braces at ground level to hold them in position.

9 Anchoring the posts. Mix concrete and pour it into each footing hole, using enough to fill beneath the post and at least 6 inches up the sides. Tamp the wet concrete to remove air pockets. Let the concrete set for 24 to 48 hours, then remove the temporary supports. Fill the rest of the hole with soil, remove the diagonal brace from the top of the deck and reinstall it underneath.

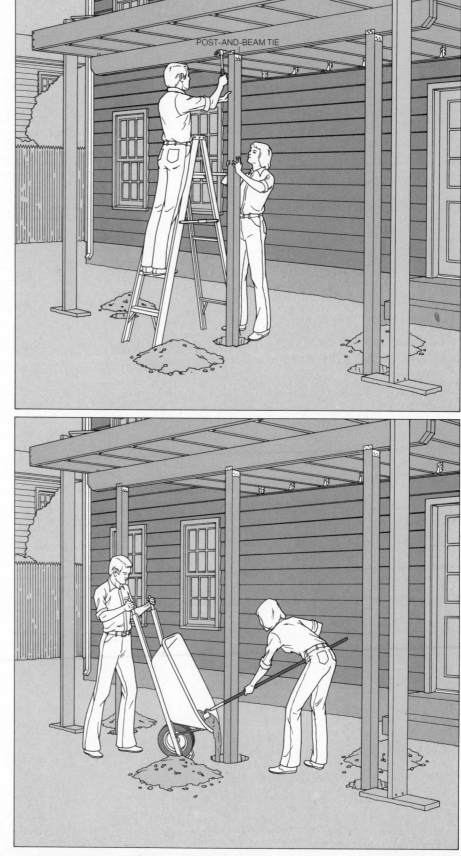

POST-AND-BEAM TIE

Simple Decking

1 Nailing down the first board. Put silicone caulking compound in the joint between the ledger and the house siding, then lay a 2-by-6 trimmed to the exact width of the deck next to the house wall. Space it slightly away from the wall if the siding is wood; fasten this first board to each joist with two nails. If the deck is too wide for a single board to span, use two lengths, joining them at the midpoint of a joist. Position subsequent boards to overhang the edge of the deck; they can all be trimmed at once later. Leave ⅛ inch between boards; the blade of a brickset makes a convenient spacer. Alternate joints when more than one length of board is needed, but always center the joint over a joist.

2 Straightening a bowed board. Position the convex edge of a bowed board against the straight edge of a previously installed board. Nail one end to a joist in the usual way; then insert a brickset at the center of the bow, and note the distance between the two decking boards at the other end. This is the amount they are out of alignment. Hold the free end of the board above the joist by the amount of misalignment, and toenail at a 45° angle through its outer edge into the joist. (The nail should enter the joist at a point closer to the house than where it would if the board were being nailed flat.) Continue hammering the nail, drawing the bowed board toward the straight board, so that by the time the nail is completely driven the gap between the two board ends has narrowed to the desired ⅛ inch. Then nail down the once-bowed board in the usual fashion. Remove the brickset.

3 Trimming the excess. Snap a chalk line above the edges of the deck onto the tops of the deck boards. Cut along the chalk line with a circular saw. Set the saw blade just deep enough to cut through the boards, watching the blade as it moves along the edge of the deck frame, to make sure it does not cut into the frame.

If you wish, and especially for cedar or redwood decking, add ¾-inch-thick fascia boards (*page 17*) to hide the ribbon board, the end joists and the cut ends of the decking. Set the upper edge of the fascia flush with the decking.

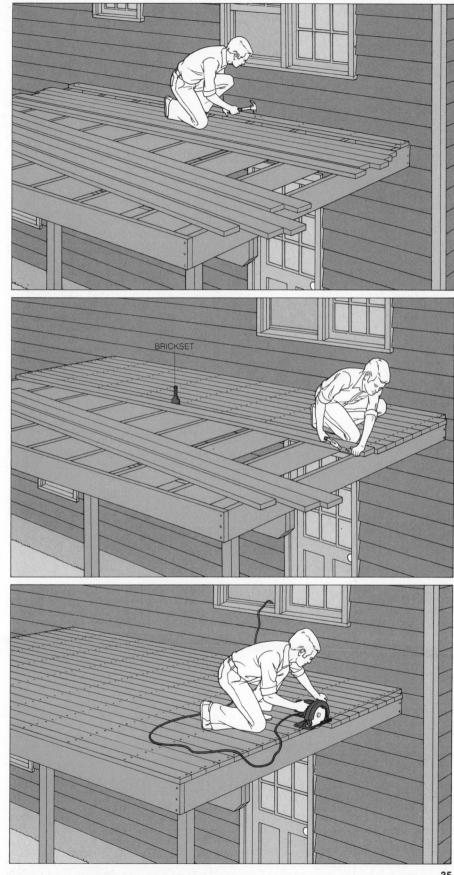

BRICKSET

Decking Alternatives

A diagonal pattern. Lay the first board of a diagonal decking pattern (*inset*) so that it crosses the ribbon board and one end joist equidistant from a corner of the frame; mark the frame first to indicate this distance. Nail the decking board to each joist with two nails; leave the ends of the board free, to be trimmed later as on page 35, Step 3, when all boards are in place. Space the boards ⅛ inch apart, as in Step 1, page 35.

When a board butts against the side of the house, cut off its end at a 45° angle before laying it. If the board also crosses the end joist at the house wall, cut a second 45° angle, perpendicular to the first. When more than one decking board is needed to span the frame, join the two boards at a joist, trimming their ends at a 45° angle to meet at the midpoint of the joist.

A herringbone pattern. To form a herringbone pattern, lay two diagonal patterns at a right angle (*inset*). Select a joist to serve as a central spine for the herringbone, adding an extra joist if none exists at the desired location. Lay the first side of the herringbone as shown above, allowing the boards to overhang the central joist until all are laid. Then snap a chalk line down the floorboards, directly over the midpoint of the central joist, and trim the boards with a circular saw set to the exact depth of the boards.

Lay the second side of the herringbone as you did the first, but trim the board ends along the central joist at a 45° angle before installing them. When a board also meets the house wall, and must be precut at both ends, cut and position the end against the house wall first. Then mark the board where it meets the end of its companion board on the other side of the herringbone spine, and make the second diagonal cut.

A Standard Railing

1 **Cutting the posts.** Cut 4-by-4 posts for the railing, 43½ inches tall, allowing for a span of 5 feet or less between posts and positioning posts within 2 feet of each corner. For style and safety, bevel the outer edge of the bottom of each post. To mark the bevel, draw a line 1 inch above the bottom of the post. Then cut along the line with a circular saw set at 45°.

2 **Attaching the posts.** Drill a ½-inch hole through the post, 1 inch above the bevel and slightly to the left of the center line of the post. Drill a second hole 5 inches above the bevel, slightly to the right of the center line. Drive a carriage bolt into the lower hole, and place the post against the edge of the deck in the desired location, positioning the bottom of the post 8¾ inches below the top of the deck. Strike the head of the bolt with a hammer, to mark the deck frame; drill through the frame at the mark. At the post position nearest the middle of each end joist, nail a wooden brace between the end joist and the next joist in, using lumber of the same dimensions as the joists. Bolt each post to the frame with a washer and a nut, but plumb the post before you tighten the nut. Drill through the second hole in each post, into the deck frame. Add a nut, a bolt and a washer at each hole.

3 Installing the railings. Nail three 2-by-6 railings to the posts; set one railing so that its top is flush with the top of the posts, the other two with their tops 23 inches and 11½ inches above the deck surface. To simplify this job, drive nails into the end posts, 5½ inches below each railing position; rest the railing there while you attach it. Join sections at the center of a post. At each corner, rest one section of railing in place, then butt the second section against the first and trim the end of the first board flush with the outer face of the second. You may also use four 2-by-4 railings evenly spaced. Where codes permit more than 6 inches between railings, you may use fewer boards.

4 Adding the handrail. Nail a 2-by-6 handrail to the top of the posts, letting it overhang the inner face of the top rail by ½ inch; use three nails at each post. To mark boards that will meet at a corner, rest the boards on the posts, ends overlapping, and level the upper board by sliding a 2-by-6 spacer under it at each post. Mark the points where the inside and outside edges of the boards intersect. Join these marks with a diagonal line across the face of each board, then cut the boards along the lines. Reposition the boards atop the posts, angled ends butted together, and nail the boards to each post with three nails; drive an extra nail through the handrail into the top rail every 12 inches.

A Picket Railing

Nailing the 2-by-2 pickets into place. To make a picket-pattern railing, substitute two 2-by-4 boards for the three 2-by-6 boards in the railing shown above. Nail one board flush with the top of the posts, and position the top of the other board 5½ inches above the deck. Cut 2-by-2 pickets 32½ inches long, and nail them to the railings on 7½-inch centers. Add a 2-by-8 top railing, allowing it to overhang the inside face of the pickets by ¾ inch.

A Slanted Railing

1 Making post openings in the deck. Cut openings in the decking for the posts of a slanted railing. Space the posts evenly and no more than 5 feet apart, beginning within 2 feet of each corner. Outline the openings by drawing a rectangle 3¾ inches wide and 3⅞ inches long, with one short side 1¼ inches away from the deck edge. Along the ribbon board, position each rectangle so that one long side is beside a joist. To start the cut, drill holes at a 15° angle at the corners of the rectangle, tilting the top of the drill toward the edge of the deck. Saw the long sides of the rectangle vertically with a saber saw. Then, for the shorter sides, tilt the saw to produce a 15° angled cut *(inset)*. Along the end joists, install a brace underneath the deck *(page 37, Step 2)* beside one edge of each of the openings.

2 Attaching the posts. Bolt a 4-foot-high post to the joist or the brace nearest one corner of the deck, using the method described on page 37, Step 2. To position the post, have a helper hold a carpenter's protractor, set at 15°, against the deck and the edge of the post. On the underside of the deck, align an inner corner of the post with the bottom of the joist or the brace. Install a second post at the other end of the deck in the same manner. Measure along the inner face of each post 35¾ inches up from the top of the deck, and stretch a chalk line between the marks. Then install the remaining posts along that side, aligning their inner faces with the chalk line. Cut the posts off level at the height of the chalk line. Repeat this procedure to attach posts to the remaining sides of the deck.

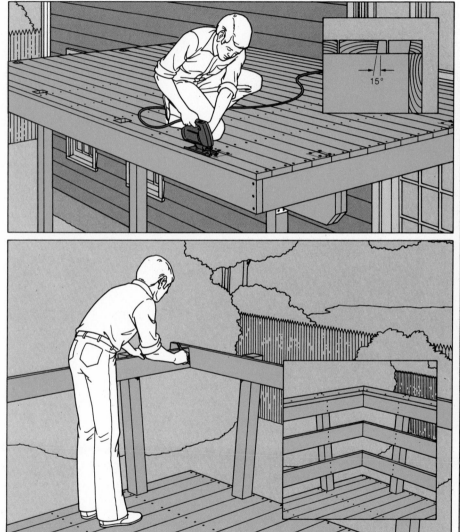

CARPENTER'S PROTRACTOR

3 Adding the railings. Drive support nails 5⅞, 17⅝ and 29⅜ inches from the top of the posts, to position 2-by-6 railings. At each level, butt the first railing board against the side of the house, its far end extending beyond the corner of the deck. Butt the adjoining railing board against it, and mark the first board where the second board touches its lower inner edge. Mark the lower edge of the second board 3 inches from the end. Remove the boards, and extend cutting lines upward from the marks, using a carpenter's protractor set to 14½° and angled to make the upper edge of each board longer. Then cut the board with a circular saw set to 44°, so that the outer face of each board is longer than the inner one. Nail the first board against the posts, and repeat the fitting procedure for subsequent corners. After all the railing boards are attached to posts, nail the boards together at the corners, driving nails into their ends from both directions. Install a handrail in the same way as for an upright railing *(Step 4, opposite)*.

Add-on Options

Simple modifications and additions to the basic structure of a deck permit you to adapt it to almost any situation or whim. Stairs connect a second-story deck to the yard. A ledger board extending past the corner of the house opens up another view and provides a point of attachment for a wraparound deck. A ledger board fastened to the studs of a house wall instead of to a joist allows the deck to project from the house at any level you choose. And by shortening some joists and joining them with angled ribbon boards, you can shape a deck edge just as you please.

Incorporating modifications calls for extra thought at the planning stage, especially for stairways. If there is to be a stairway landing—as most codes require for stairs that descend more than 8 feet—the height of the landing must be based on a multiple of 7¼ inches, the height of a riser. Begin the measurement from the top of the frame, not the decking. And the distance of the landing from the deck will be governed by the number of risers, multiplied by 10¾ inches—the width of an average tread—with 15 inches subtracted from the result so that half the bottom tread extends over the landing. If these calculations put the landing at an awkward place, you may elect to modify the deck plans.

It is best to build stairs and landing before adding railings to the deck, because the railing posts for the deck can often support the stair railings as well. Sometimes, in fact, the deck posts can be extended downward to support the railings of the stairs, as shown on page 30.

2 **Adding an angled corner board.** Set a circular saw to cut a 45° angle, and cut the corner board at the marks so that the outer face of the board will be longer than the inner one. Position the board against the cut ends of the end joist and ribbon board, and nail the board in place.

By cutting the frame elsewhere along the deck edge, you can create different shapes. Shortening a joist near the midpoint of an edge and adding angled ribbon boards creates a notch. Cutting the joists progressively shorter from two corners of the deck out to the midpoint of one edge approximates a curve (inset).

Shaping Cutaway Corners

1 **Cutting the frame.** To shape the corners or edges of a deck, construct the frame in the usual fashion (pages 31-34), then cut away portions according to the shape you want. For an angled corner, make a cutting mark on the end joist between the outside corner and the supporting beam, then make a mark on the ribbon board at the same distance from the corner. Cut the two boards at the marks you have just made, removing the corner of the frame. Measure the distance between the outside edges of the cut frame members (inset), and transfer this measurement to a corner board that is the same lumber size as the frame members.

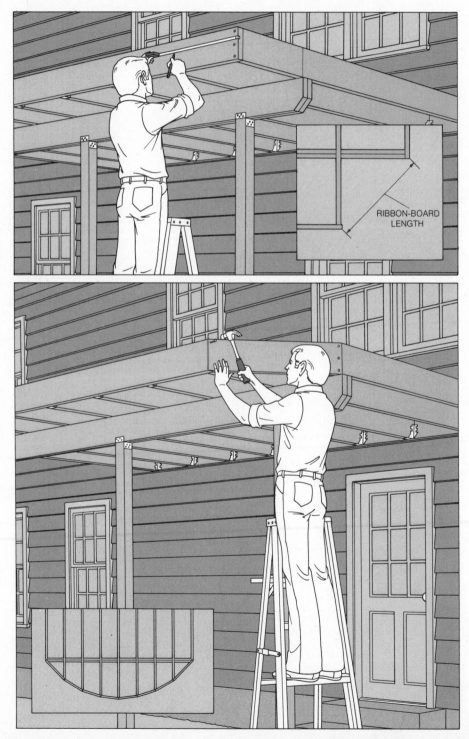

RIBBON-BOARD LENGTH

3 **Fitting an angled railing.** After the decking is installed, add 4-by-4 railing posts around the edge of the deck as in Steps 1 and 2, page 37, using at least two posts for each section of deck, no matter how short the section. Drive nails to support railings along each section, as in Step 3, page 38, then mark the railing boards for corner joints. Rest a board on its supporting nails, outer end extending beyond the deck. Hold the board for the other railing underneath it, resting the second board against its two posts. Mark where the two boards intersect along both their inner and their outer faces, and draw guidelines across the edges of the boards, connecting the two points. Extend a squared line down the inner face of each board, and cut along it with a circular saw set to match the angled guidelines. Replace the first board, and nail it on.

Butt the cut end of the second board against the first, and mark the cutting lines for the next corner joint. Add a handrail as on page 38.

Adding a Stairway

FACING BOARD

1 **Building the steps.** Cut the stair carriages as on page 16, Step 2, with risers 7¼ inches high and treads 10¾ inches deep. Extend the depth of the next-to-last tread to allow for the thickness of the frame; if your framing lumber is larger than a 2-by-8, notch the back of the next-to-last tread to fit around it. Extend the last tread to the end of the carriage. Use a carriage as a template for marking the ends of two facing boards. Nail up the carriages, butting the last riser against the back of the frame; then nail the facing boards to the carriages and the frame. Add treads made of pairs of 2-by-6 boards, nailing through the facing board into the treads.

2 **Trimming the post tops.** Bolt 4-by-4 railing posts, 4 feet long, to the carriage assemblies as in Step 2, page 37. Position the top posts flush with the edge of the deck. Space additional posts no more than 5 feet apart, with the bottom post near the bottom of the carriage. Set the bottom of each post so that the edge nearest the deck is aligned with the bottom of the carriage. Mark the tops of the posts to match the angle of the stairway; to do this, slide the 16-inch arm of a steel square along the top of the facing board while holding a pencil at the end of the 24-inch arm. Saw along the lines with a circular saw, a handsaw or, if necessary, both.

3 **Cutting the railings.** Drive supporting nails for the railing boards as in Step 3, page 38, and temporarily tack a top railing board into position. Mark the back of the board where it meets the upper edge of the top post and the lower edge of the bottom post. Remove the board, cut the ends, then nail the board in place. Repeat for all the rest of the railing boards.

4 **Fitting the handrail.** Rest a 2-by-6 handrail board on the upper railing, allowing it to project about 4 inches beyond the post at the bottom of the stairs. Mark the side of the board where it meets the upper and lower edges of the top post, and draw lines at these marks across the top of the board. Then shift the board onto the top of the lower posts, outer edge of the board flush with the outer edge of the posts. Butt the board against the top post, and draw a line down the face of the board even with the inner face of the post. Cut a notch at the marked lines (*inset*).

Mark and notch the opposite handrail board in the same way. Trim off the bottom corners of the handrails, if desired, and nail the handrails to the posts and top railings.

Dig around and under the ends of the stair carriage 4 inches deep. Prop the ends up on small stones so that the stair treads are level, then pour a concrete footing as on page 16, Step 1.

Enlarging the Deck Area

Extending a ledger board. A deck that extends beyond the corner of a house needs a ledger board that extends similarly. The ledger must be plumb, which means that on a clapboard house you will have to rest it on the points of the siding or shim it to keep it upright. In addition, the ledger extension will require structural support. If the extension is part of a wraparound deck, the beam of the adjacent deck section will provide this support. If the deck extension stands alone and does not project beyond the house more than 6 feet, you can just double the entire ledger board, in effect creating a cantilevered beam. If the deck does extend beyond the house more than 6 feet, the ledger will need supporting posts within 2 feet of its outer end and at 8-foot intervals in between. When posts support the extension, only the projecting section of the ledger needs to be doubled.

Attaching a ledger between floors. For a multilevel deck or a deck with stairs and a landing, at least one ledger is likely to be between floors of the house. A masonry wall will support a ledger anywhere, but on a wood-frame house you will have to bolt the ledger to the studs.

To probe inside the wall for the studs, drill a series of small holes at the level of the ledger, until the drill bit hits a solid surface behind the sheathing. Then drill a number of small holes close together around that point, to locate the edges of the stud. Mark the midpoint of the stud on the wall of the house; then mark the midpoints of other studs—they usually are 16 inches apart. Caulk the probe holes but do not bother to hide them: They will be covered by the ledger. Attach the ledger as shown on page 12, Step 1.

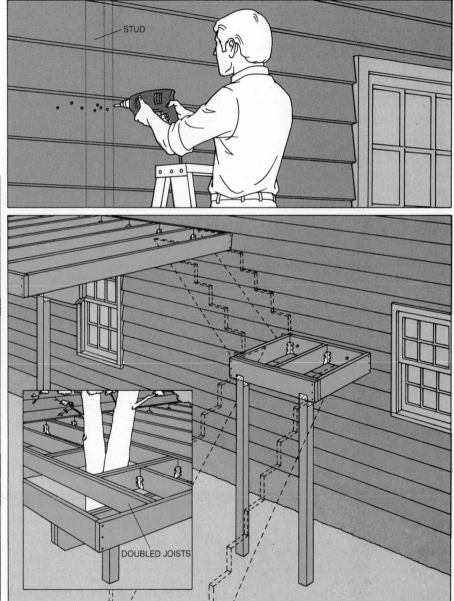

Building a landing. A landing is a miniature deck having a doubled ribbon board in lieu of a beam, with two end joists and as many intermediate joists as needed to maintain a joist spacing of 2 feet or less. As part of a staircase, a landing can rest on its own ledger board and on posts attached to the doubled ribbon board. Stairways are then added from the ground and to the deck. If the ledger board is replaced by a second doubled ribbon board, the landing can stand free on four posts.

You can also fasten a landing to the ledger supporting a deck, or to flanking decks *(page 30)*. Finally, to surround a tree *(inset)*, attach landings to the ledger in back and the ribbon board in front. When a landing is next to a deck joist, double that joist and omit the landing's end joist.

Repairing Weatherworn Posts and Floors

Exposure to the outdoors eventually takes its toll on wood porches or decks. Both are particularly vulnerable to dampness and insect infestation.

Moisture, which fosters the growth of wood-rotting fungi and bacteria, becomes trapped in joints and between floorboards and is absorbed by the end grain of cut boards. Moisture may also collect around the bottom of porch and deck posts, and it can be absorbed directly from the earth wherever wood meets the ground. Wood-boring insects are even more destructive, gnawing through critical structural members and even reaching the roof of a porch.

To catch damage by these natural enemies of wood in its early stages and avoid the need for extensive repairs, inspect your porch or deck periodically. Spongy and discolored wood is an indication of rot; little piles of wood fibers or shed wings are signs of insect activity. If insects are present, exterminate them before beginning any repair work.

If rot or insect damage is widespread, it may be necessary to replace the entire porch or deck; but in most cases you can patch the structure by removing and replacing damaged supports or damaged sections of supports (pages 44-46). Individual floorboards can also be replaced (page 47), and weakened joists reinforced (page 46). To retard future damage, always replace deck and porch parts with pressure-treated lumber, and use galvanized nails and anchors in order to prevent rust.

Before replacing a post or a column, first take the weight off it by bracing the structure that it supports with a screw-operated, telescoping jack. Or, to support low decks or porch floors, use a bell jack—a strong, bell-shaped screw jack about 1 foot tall. (You can increase a bell jack's working height by inserting a cut-to-fit length of 4-by-4 between it and the structure.) Both jacks are available at lumberyards and from tool-rental dealers. Do not use hydraulic jacks; they are not as reliable as the screw type.

In preparation for using a jack, grease its threads; then pad it at the bottom with a 2-foot length of 2-by-12 scrap lumber and at the top with a 1-foot length of 2-by-6, to distribute the load. If you are jacking a deck or a porch floor, place the bottom pad on the ground and level it before extending the jack. Always position the jack directly below the beam or header joist supported by the post you are removing, and as close as possible to the post. If you are jacking a porch roof, place the jack directly over a beam or joist on which the floor rests, to support the weight transferred to the jack.

In replacing a post that holds up a deck or porch floor, you will usually be dealing with a concrete footing. If the post is attached to the top of its footing with a metal post anchor, simply unbolt the damaged post and install a new one. But if the base of the post is embedded in the concrete, you will have to modify the footing before installing a new post.

The modificatons will vary with the footing. If the top of the footing is at or near ground level, you can dig out the embedded wood, fill the cavity with concrete and install a post anchor (opposite, bottom). If the top of the footing is more than 8 inches below ground, remove as much of the wood as possible, then pour a new footing over the old one. Sometimes, if only a section of post is rotted, you can simply cut out the damaged area, splicing in a new section (page 46).

In replacing a traditional round porch column, you will first have to see if it is solid or hollow; to do this, drill into it in at least two places. A solid column is removed in the same way as a post. Inside a hollow column there usually is a post that supports the roof; if this inner support is sound, you need only replace the outer shell (opposite, top right).

After the repair is complete, several measures can prevent a recurrence of the trouble. If your porch or deck is painted, periodically scrape and repaint blistered and cracked sections that can trap moisture. If it is unpainted and is not made of pressure-treated lumber, treat it once a year with a preservative such as pentachlorophenol or copper naphthenate. Keep the floor of a wood porch or deck swept clean of moisture-retaining leaves, and repair roof leaks promptly.

Removing Porch Posts and Columns

1 **Jacking a porch roof.** Set the jack on a 2-by-12 pad, lining it up between a floor joist and the roof header joist; lock the jack's telescoping tubes in the position that brings the top tube about 2 inches from the roof header joist, using the steel pins provided. While a helper holds the jack plumb and steadies a second pad between the jack and the roof header joist, raise the jack by turning the screw handle. When the jack is snug against the pads, give the handle another quarter turn, just enough for the jack to support the roof without lifting it.

2 **Disassembling the support.** To remove a porch post or a solid column (*below, left*), use a handsaw to make two crosscuts, about 1 foot apart, through the wood. Knock out the middle section with a mallet, and work the top and bottom sections loose. Install a new post as shown on page 20, Steps 2-4.

To remove a hollow column (*below, right*), make two vertical cuts opposite each other down the length of the shaft, using a circular saw. Make a horizontal cut around the middle. Pull the two upper sections apart and remove them, staying clear of the capital if it falls—it may not be nailed to the header. Cut the capital in two

with a saber saw or a handsaw, and detach it from the support post. If the capital is attached to the header, free it with a pry bar. Remove the two lower shaft sections and the base. Check the inner support post to see if it is damaged; replace it if necessary. Cover the post with a new shaft, capital and base.

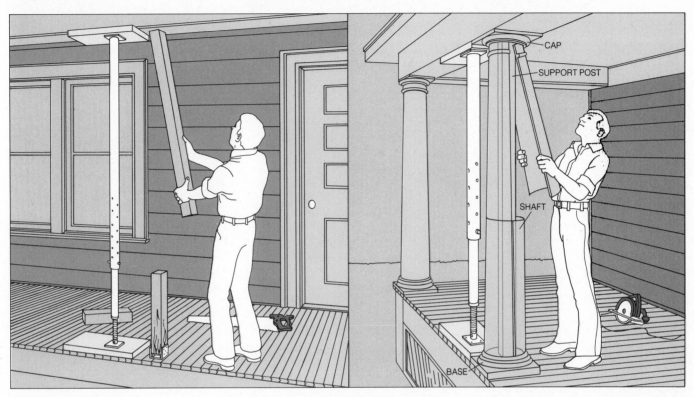

Salvaging the Usable Parts of a Deck Support

Reusing a ground-level footing. When the damaged post for a porch or deck floor rests on a concrete footing near ground level, sink a J-shaped anchor bolt in the footing to secure a post anchor as the base for a new post. To prepare the footing, jack up the floor, cut off the damaged post flush with the top of the footing and pry out the rotted wood with a wood chisel. Fill the footing cavity with new concrete, sink the anchor bolt in it and attach the post anchor (*inset*), establishing its position by hanging a plumb bob from the floor beam where the top of the post will be fastened. When the concrete has cured for 24 to 48 hours, cut a new post to fit between the floor beam and the post anchor. Nail it to the post anchor and fasten it to the beam, using the original hardware.

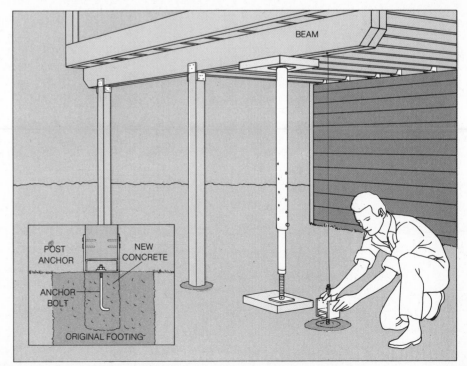

Building up a buried footing. When a damaged post for a deck or porch floor rests on a concrete footing that is well below ground level, build up the footing as a base for the new post. To prepare the new footing, jack up the floor, dig down to expose the entire top of the old footing and cut off the damaged post as close as possible to the top of the old footing. Fill in the hole with concrete, covering the remnants of the old post by at least 8 inches. Measure and cut a new post long enough to sink into the new footing about 1 inch, and lower it into the concrete. Hold the post plumb while a helper fastens it at the top with the same hardware used on the old post. Brace the bottom of the post with scrap lumber *(inset),* to hold the post plumb until the concrete has set.

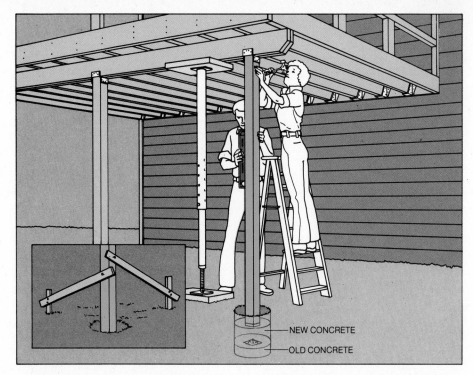

NEW CONCRETE

OLD CONCRETE

A Splice for a Weak Post

Replacing part of a post. When only the upper or lower part of a porch or deck post is rotten, you can splice in a new section instead of replacing the whole post. Jack up the floor or roof, and saw the post in two just beyond the damaged area. Measure and cut a replacement section, taking into account the change in length if a new footing is needed *(above).* Cut an L-shaped notch, half the thickness of the post and 6 inches long, in the end of the undamaged section, and a matching notch in one end of the replacement section. Clamp the notched sections together, and counterbore three ⅜-inch holes through the joint, staggering their positions. Secure the joint with ⅜-inch carriage bolts. Then attach the other end of the replacement section to the header joist.or to the footing.

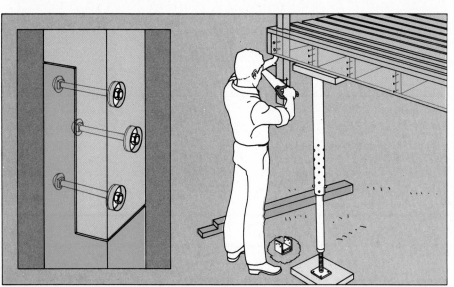

Reinforcing a damaged joist. To brace a weak joist, fasten a matching joist against it. Have a helper hold the new joist against the old, flush with the floorboards, while you secure its two ends to the ledger board and header with 7-inch galvanized angle plates held by fourpenny (1½-inch) nails. Then nail the two joists together with 16-penny (3½-inch) nails, staggered top and bottom at 12-inch intervals. Then nail the floorboards to the top edge of the new joist.

If the old joist sags, jack it until its bottom edge is level with the new joist, and leave the jack in place until the two joists are nailed together.

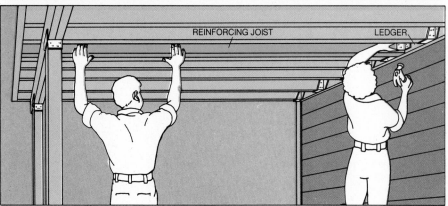

REINFORCING JOIST

LEDGER

Patching a Tongue-and-Groove Floor

1 **Chiseling the damaged floorboards.** Use a 1-inch wood chisel to make cuts across both ends of each floorboard in the damaged section. To make each cut, first drive the chisel straight down, holding it so that the beveled edge faces the damaged part of the board. Then reverse the chisel, pointing it at an angle toward the cut that you have just made, and make a second cut, chipping out a deep groove. Center all of these cuts over the joists, and stagger them in such a way that no two adjoining floorboards are cut over the same joist.

2 **Removing the boards.** With a circular saw set to the thickness of the floor, make two parallel cuts down the middle of the longest damaged board, starting and stopping the saw just short of the chiseled ends. Complete the saw cuts with a wood chisel, then lift out the middle strip with a pry bar. Working first on the grooved side, then on the tongued side, pry out the rest of the board, using the pry bar to loosen the nails at the joists. Pry out the other damaged boards, using the opening left by the removal of an adjacent board as leverage space.

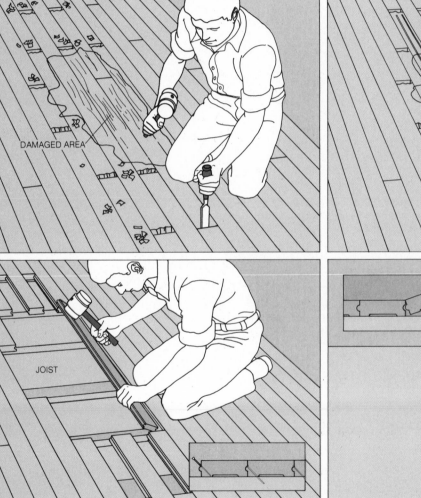

DAMAGED AREA

JOIST

3 **Inserting new boards.** Wedge a replacement board into position, fitting its grooved edge over the tongue of the undamaged adjacent board. Use a rubber mallet to force the new board into place. Then drive eightpenny (2½-inch) finishing nails through the corner of its tongue into the joists below *(inset)*. Install as many boards as possible this way. For any pieces that cannot be wedged into place, use the alternate joining method described in Step 4.

4 **Installing the final boards.** When there is not enough maneuvering space to slide a replacement board into position, trim off the lower lip of its grooved edge with a chisel. Engage its tongued edge in the groove of the adjacent board, and drop its trimmed edge into place *(inset)*, tapping it gently with a rubber mallet in order to seat it. Then face-nail the board at each joist with two eightpenny finishing nails, set at an angle, and fill the nail holes with wood putty.

Reviving a Genteel Tradition

Porch, piazza, veranda, gallery—call it what you will, there is no architectural element potentially more pleasing to mind and body than this old-fashioned indoor-outdoor room with a view.

Set on the street side of a house in town, the front porch offers the ideal vantage from which to watch the world go by. Oriented toward a fine landscape, the porch invites front-row participation in an ever-changing experience of nature. Grafted onto the back of a house, adjoining a secluded garden or in the shade of a massive tree, it becomes an indolent retreat in which to read a book, take a snooze, sip a long cool drink or entertain friends. And everywhere it is a convenient, sheltered place to lean back and stretch out the legs while getting acquainted with the day. In short, a porch is a pretty fine place for a lot of things, as the following portfolio of traditional and modern versions illustrates.

While not strictly an American invention, porches have enjoyed unique favor in our residential architecture almost from the start. Perhaps they are an outgrowth of our love for the great outdoors. Perhaps, as some architectural historians have proposed, they are tangible expressions of national character—outward-looking, pragmatic, informal.

The first porch designs seem to have been imported to the Deep South in the 18th Century from France by way of the West Indies. By the mid-19th Century, their merit in moderating the Southern climate established, they were bursting forth from New Orleans to Quebec. By Victorian times, porches were deemed so essential that they carried most of the burden of architectural style. As houses rose heavenward, all a-bristle with turrets, crockets, finials, towers and spires, they were routinely brought back to earth on the spreading wings of wide porches with deep, overhanging eaves.

Excesses of the Victorian era—too many deep-set porches made many houses dark inside—contributed to the porch's temporary decline in the 20th Century. So did air conditioning and, very likely, cars and television, which changed the way Americans relaxed. But the pendulum on energy use and home amusement is swinging back again, and along with it the porch.

Developments in translucent building materials, as shown on page 55, are making it possible to build porches that do not greatly reduce interior light. The trend toward smaller houses also makes the idea of having a convertible, indoor-outdoor room appealing. As shown on page 52, an existing porch can in many climates be winterized with relatively little structural work. If it is also blessed with a southern exposure, the winterized porch becomes a passive solar collector, pumping the heat of midday to the adjoining rooms.

Older houses may offer less choice of solutions than new ones, but the rewards in architectural effect are as great if not greater. The new owners of the house opposite were fortunate in inheriting a porch whose basic elements remained sound; the main work involved was stripping and repainting. Other owners of old houses start with a dwelling that has lost its porches during an earlier streamlining, in which case the choice is between rebuilding precisely along original lines or starting fresh.

If the house has a distinctive architectural character, or if a porch could restore the character the house once had, the most successful approach generally is to approximate the scale, ornamentation and materials of the original. Research in pattern books, in old photographs, and in houses of the same vintage can resolve most questions. Old houses that date from pre-porch times (18th Century New England houses, for example) present a different challenge. Sometimes the best solution is to incorporate the porch into the framework of the original building, a style that actually has historic validity, as the example on page 51 illustrates.

Wood turner's pride and joy. Looking like a page from an artisan's sample book, this wondrous display of Victorian fancywork frames the porch of a Southern town house (page 50). Like the rest of the structure, the porch dates from 1899, but all its spools, spindles, balusters, newel posts and pillars remain in good condition. The sweeping C curves are cut from flat stock and connected with almost invisible joinery.

Southern confection. Designed chiefly for sheer visual delight, these deep-set double galleries also provide ample protection from the hot Georgia sun.

Porches That Contribute to the Design of the House

Back in the 19th Century, when porches were common features of almost every new American dwelling, there was a happy tendency to explore their architectural as well as practical possibilities. Not only could porches provide a measure of shelter in warm weather; they could yield year-round benefits in terms of a house's exterior appearance, dignifying an entrance, lending an ever-changing play of light and shade to an entire façade.

In the example at left, a pair of extraordinarily high-spirited porches embellishes an otherwise plain street front. The beach-front cottage at right is banded by a series of low porches that marry the faceted structure to its site. A sensitive solution for a town house on a small lot is the indented porch shown below.

Wraparound porches. A rhythmic sequence of shallow-roofed arcades and white-painted railings plays horizontal counterpoint to a lofty assemblage of turrets, peaks, angles and arches in this Shingle-style summer cottage.

Small setback. This small back porch, set into a house dating from the 1840s, is designed to provide privacy, shelter and a fine overview of the garden, while retaining the classic rectilinear frame of the architectural period.

Purposeful Spaces: Outdoor Rooms to Relax In

Like alpine herdsmen, many Americans migrate to summer quarters when the weather beckons, leaving the confines of their indoor life to spend most of their waking—and perhaps some of their sleeping—hours on the porch. Such outdoor rooms need adroit planning to fulfill all of the demands placed upon them. They must take advantage of prevailing breezes, sun exposure, proximity to the kitchen (if outdoor dining and entertaining are to be part of the regular agenda) and outlook.

Two countrified spaces *(left and below)* and a vine-roofed extension to a city penthouse *(opposite)* represent three adaptations to living with a degree of luxury on the edge of the great outdoors.

All-season conservatory. Within wood frames that take screens in summer, insulated glass in winter, this brick-floored porch functions year-round as a second living room. White wicker and cheerful cotton prints keep the mood informal.

Lake Huron prospect. A broad view, mirrored in the windows, dictates the arrangement of furnishings on this traditional veranda with blue ceiling and floor.

Pseudo porch. A white-painted railing encloses an area of a rooftop terrace for alfresco dining, under a seasonal canopy of wisteria.

Porches That Add without Subtracting

Enjoying all the benefits of a porch without sacrificing natural light in the adjoining interiors may sound like having your cake and eating it too, but as the options on this and the following pages show, both are possible.

Below, a breezeway takes off at a right angle to the house wall, and light still reaches the inside. A second possibility *(top right)* is a relatively shallow porch, just wide enough to damp the noonday sun and keep the rain off the rocker.

Other options exploit new translucent roofing materials *(below right),* or the screening effects of a porch railing put to novel use *(overleaf).* Instead of rising from the floor, the railing drops from the roof line, deflecting the hottest sun and at the same time drawing together an almost too-generous space. It also looks vaguely like a reredos, in keeping with the ecclesiastical details.

Covered bridge. A raised passage-breezeway is framed trellis-style with Douglas fir posts, joists and deck. Discrete fiberglass panels atop it shed the weather.

Mainstreet lookout. Wide enough to keep its occupants out of the rain, narrow enough for them to see and be seen, this pared-down porch does a limited job very well—and without depriving the windows along the back wall of their own place in the sun.

Transparent treehouse. To increase the usefulness of a generous-sized deck without shadowing the adjoining kitchen, a section has been enclosed with a tent of screening and rigid plastic. An obliquely angled outer wall that parallels the deck's outer edge, and wood framing that blends into the board-and-batten siding of the house, are some of the devices that help this addition settle naturally into place.

Sunstruck vestry. In a former church, the solid wall of what was once a vestry room has been opened up to create a broad, bright, airy veranda.

The Sleeping-Porch Panacea

"Tight sleeping rooms," warned *The American Woman's Home* in 1869, "are now starving and poisoning more than one-half of this nation."

To that awful admonition, Harriet Beecher Stowe added some grisly details: Stagnant air in America's homes was breeding "slow-creeping, black blood which clogs the brain and lies like a weight on the vital wheels!"

Stowe wrote of the unfortunate child who "this morning sits up in bed with his hair bristling with crossness, strikes at his nurse and declares he won't say his prayers." Her diagnosis: "The child, having slept in a close box of a room, his brain all night fed by poison, is in a mild state of moral insanity."

By the turn of the century, however, Victorian society had found a cure for its contaminated lungs—fresh air—and it had enthusiastically embraced the sleeping porch. "This most modern mode of living is sure to become universal in this country and this century," wrote a convert in 1913.

For the next quarter century, the sleeping porch ranked as the most desired and most specialized room in the house. Buyers of new homes demanded sleeping porches, and homeowners adapted existing porches for sleeping.

Several powerful and simultaneous factors accounted for this nightly exodus into the open air. The nation was straining at its Victorian laces, rebelling against close, dark Victorian homes. With the new century came a wave of nostalgia for earlier times, for a connection with the vanishing frontier. Teddy Roosevelt, riding this wave, added the luster of the presidency to the movement by espousing porch sleeping.

Finally, a frightening tuberculosis epidemic galvanized Americans into health consciousness. The country adopted strict new sanitation laws, required pasteurization of milk and built a network of tuberculosis sanatoriums in rural

Fresh-air folly. The sleeping porch led one inventor to patent this disappearing bed.

areas—away from polluted city air. Indeed, such was the commitment to fresh air that entire families foreswore their bedrooms to sleep barracks-style on the porch, cot against cot.

Logically, the sleeping porch was often placed on the second floor, usually above another porch, to be near dressing rooms and to capture the "purer" air at that height. As a concession to climate, the homeowner might screen the porch, and thwart rain and snow (and the gaze of neighbors) by hanging curtains of khaki or duck.

To unclutter the sleeping porch by day, industrious inventors rigged beds that would fold and store out of sight. One such sliding bed *(above)*, patented in 1913, rolled fully made through an opening in the wall of the house, onto the porch: The footboard of the bed fitted snugly into the opening, to seal it. The designer of this bed suggested that it be housed indoors in a heated and ventilated metal case that could double

as a convenient platform for the piano.

The greatest challenge lay in sleeping outdoors in the winter. *The Book of Little Houses,* published in 1914, suggested the following order for assembling the bed: a layer of newspapers atop the mattress, six layers of woolen blankets, three pairs of wool and cotton blankets, a comforter, a tightly woven bedspread, and a waterproof cloth that was to be attached to the foot of the bed and suspended from hooks above the sleeper's head. For the sleeper, the book prescribed "underclothes, flannel pajamas, worsted stockings (or bed slippers) and a worsted hood tied tightly under the chin."

Shortly thereafter Americans abandoned the sleeping porch, along with the waterproof cloths and the worsted hoods, for another architectural status symbol. With the advent of the motor car, middle-class homeowners hastened to acquire the newest sign of social rank: the garage.

2 Masonry Floors That Float

Sinuous bricks. Resting on a bed of tamped sand, these interlocking paving bricks are simply tapped into place with a rubber mallet, and they stay that way even when rain water freezes and expands in the cracks between them. Their zigzagging sides secure them against one another, preventing them from shifting in any direction, and for added visual effect, they create patterns on the floor of the patio.

A patio paved with brick, tile or stone has a lot to recommend it. Unlike wood flooring, these masonry materials do not rot or burn, and they last for many years. Their installation cost can be less than that of wood, especially when they are laid on a bed of sand. But even when laid over a concrete base, a masonry patio need not be expensive, as long as the site does not require unusually extensive preparation and you do not go overboard in the choice of materials.

Despite their apparent solidity, masonry surfaces actually float on the surface of the ground, rising and subsiding with spring thaws and winter frosts. In the case of concrete, the entire slab floats on an underlayer of gravel, while bricks and stones embedded in sand shift their positions individually to adapt to the ground's changing contours. Indeed, after a particularly severe winter, sand-laid paving blocks offer the advantage of being easily taken up and reset.

Site preparation for the underlayer of gravel or sand can often be the most important step in building a paved patio. The ground must be smooth and gently graded, to prevent water from collecting in pockets beneath the surface. Sometimes, on a hilly site, the grading involves extensive reshaping of the land. A rented rotary tiller can simplify this task. If the ground falls away very steeply, you may, in addition, prefer to create a series of small terraced patios instead of a single large one—thus minimizing the earth-moving process.

In preparing the site, you will also want to consider the presence of a favorite shade tree—whose roots, stretching out as far as the tips of the branches, should be disturbed as little as possible. A heavy layer of soil topped by a concrete slab will smother that root system, depriving it of air and water. Conversely, the tree roots, pushing up to the surface in search of air and water, can destroy the paving.

If you want a tree and a patio to coexist peacefully, choose a paving material that can be laid in sand, so that water can trickle down between the bricks or stones. In addition, leave a foot or so of open space around the trunk of the tree, and regularly give the tree an extra ration of water— preferably with a deep-root feeder—so that the roots will be encouraged to stay well below the patio surface.

In choosing a paving material, consider the cost of moving it from its point of origin to your site. Stones, bricks, tiles and concrete are heavy. The price of ready-mixed concrete may, for example, be 40 per cent more in Atlanta than it is in Dallas or San Francisco, which are nearer to sources of portland cement and gravel aggregate. Tiles and bricks are likely to be cheaper where there are extensive clay deposits, and flagstone is cheaper near slate quarries. Using an indigenous material has another advantage: It may result in a patio whose colors and textures blend more harmoniously into the landscape.

Laying the Foundation for a Concrete Slab

A concrete slab, free-form or rectangular, is the solid base of many a porch and patio. Used alone, it provides a versatile outdoor living area in countless backyards. But it can also serve as a vehicle for decorative surface treatments—exposed pebbles, striations, set-in wooden discs— or as an underpinning for bricks *(page 80)* or unglazed clay tiles *(page 88)*. Supported by masonry footings and piers, a concrete slab will even carry the columns of a heavy porch roof *(page 18)*.

No matter what purpose a slab is intended to serve, its actual pouring should be preceded by careful planning. Local zoning laws may dictate the location, design and dimensions of a slab, and building codes often specify its thickness, as well as its degree of slope for water run-off. Generally slabs are required to be 4 to 6 inches thick, depending on the local climate, and to slope away from a house ¼ to ⅛ inch per foot.

Your planning will also be influenced by the nature of your site—especially the stability of the ground. If there is recent landfill more than 3 feet deep, you may have problems with settling, as you may also have if water is found within 1 foot of the surface. If such conditions exist, seek the advice of a landscape architect. Professional help is also advisable if you live in an earthquake zone.

In deciding on the location of the slab, consider the presence of any obstacles to excavation, such as trees and shrubs, gas, electric, water or sewer lines, or dry wells, septic tanks or cesspools. Decide whether you want to have a sunny or shady patio and take into account existing pathways around the house. Then measure all the relevant distances and make a scale drawing that shows existing structures and landscape features.

When the plan is completed, the site preparation can begin. Lay out boundaries for the slab with wood stakes and string, and set up grade lines to ensure that the slab, when poured, will have the proper slope. Then install form boards and expansion joints.

Expansion joints consist of strips of asphalt-impregnated joint filler. They separate the slab from any rigid structure that abuts it, and subdivide large slabs into 8- to 10-foot squares. Not all localities require expansion joints within a slab, but if your local building code does, the joints must be placed against temporary form boards *(page 63)*.

These form boards, which contain the concrete as it is poured, are usually removed after the slab has hardened. But sometimes they remain as a permanent decorative feature. Temporary forms are usually made of smooth wood such as fir, pine or spruce, nailed together with double-headed scaffolding nails for easier dismantling. Pressure-treated redwood and cedar are the best woods for perma-

nent forms. For curved and free-form slabs, make the forms of flexible strips of ¼-inch hardboard or plywood.

The composition of the slab itself is almost always the same, regardless of its size, shape or location. At the bottom is a layer of compacted soil, usually topped by a layer of gravel. The gravel, a drainage bed, keeps the slab dry. Drainage beds vary in depth, depending on the climate, the composition of the soil, and the planned thickness of the slab. For a 4-inch slab in an average situation of moderate climate and sandy soil, the drainage bed usually consists of a 2- to 4-inch layer of ¾-inch gravel. But if the soil is rocky or has a high clay content, a 6-inch drainage bed may be needed.

The drainage bed is topped by a layer of wire mesh. The mesh is essential in regions where the soil does not compact easily; it holds the slab together when hairline cracks develop.

When the excavation is fully prepared, calculate the amount of concrete you will need. For a rectangular slab, use the chart below; for a free-form slab, use the method shown opposite to estimate the area to be covered, then refer to the chart. You can, if you like, mix the concrete yourself, using a rented mixer. But for jobs the size of a porch or a patio, it usually is better to have the concrete delivered to the site, ready-mixed, in a truck *(page 68)*.

Calculating Quantities of Gravel and Concrete

Estimating cubic yardage. To determine the amount of gravel and concrete required for a rectangular drainage bed and slab, calculate the area to be covered, in square feet. Locate the closest figure in the left-hand column of the chart at right, and read across that row to the column corresponding with the proposed thickness of the gravel bed or slab, in inches. Then add 8 per cent to the volume indicated, to compensate for waste and spillage.

Area of slab	Thickness of slab				
	2 in.	3 in.	4 in.	5 in.	6 in.
10 sq. ft.	.06 cu. yd.	.09 cu. yd.	.12 cu. yd.	.15 cu. yd.	.18 cu. yd.
25 sq. ft.	.16 cu. yd.	.24 cu. yd.	.32 cu. yd.	.4 cu. yd.	.48 cu. yd.
50 sq. ft.	.32 cu. yd.	.48 cu. yd.	.64 cu. yd.	.8 cu. yd.	.96 cu. yd.
100 sq. ft.	.64 cu. yd.	.96 cu. yd.	1.28 cu. yd.	1.6 cu. yd.	1.92 cu. yd.
200 sq. ft.	1.28 cu. yd.	1.92 cu. yd.	2.56 cu. yd.	3.2 cu. yd.	3.84 cu. yd.
300 sq. ft.	1.92 cu. yd.	2.88 cu. yd.	3.84 cu. yd.	4.8 cu. yd.	5.76 cu. yd.
400 sq. ft.	2.56 cu. yd.	3.84 cu. yd.	5.12 cu. yd.	6.4 cu. yd.	7.68 cu. yd.
500 sq. ft.	3.2 cu. yd.	4.8 cu. yd.	6.4 cu. yd.	8.0 cu. yd.	9.6 cu. yd.

Finding the area of a free-form slab. To determine the approximate area of a free-form slab, outline the slab on graph paper, with each of the squares representing 1 square foot. Assign a rough fractional value to each square partially covered by the slab. Then add up the full squares and the fractions, to find the approximate area of the proposed slab. Use this figure and the chart on page 60 to calculate the quantity of gravel and concrete you will need.

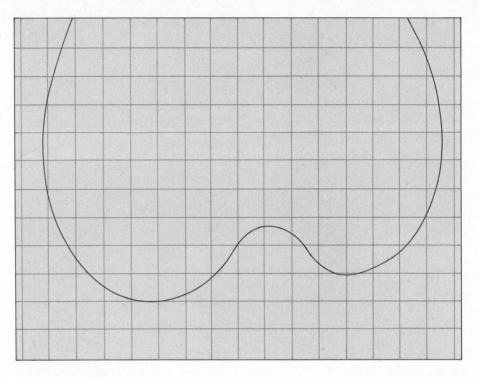

Excavating and Grading a Rectangular Slab

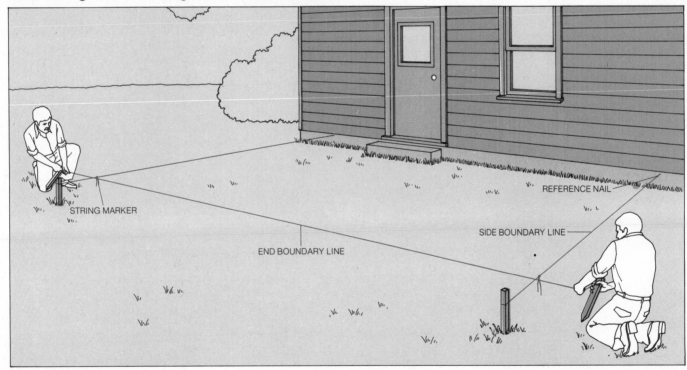

STRING MARKER

REFERENCE NAIL

SIDE BOUNDARY LINE

END BOUNDARY LINE

1 Laying out and excavating the site. Using strings that you have stretched from two reference nails driven into the wall of the house, and following the 3-4-5 method described on page 9, lay out two boundary lines for the sides of the slab, perpendicular to the house wall. Anchor the strings to two 2-by-2 stakes driven into the ground 2 feet beyond the planned length of the sides. Then measure back 2 feet from the stakes, and tie string markers around the boundary strings. Cut a third piece of string, 4 feet longer than the distance between the strings marking the side boundaries. Then, with a helper, stretch this string across the side boundary strings and perpendicular to them, lining it up with the string markers and anchoring it to two 2-by-2 stakes driven 2 feet beyond the point where the strings intersect.

To excavate the area, first dig a trench 1 foot outside the boundary lines, starting at the house wall. Work in parallel rows, back and forth between the perimeter trenches. Save sod and dirt to fill in at the sides of the finished slab.

2 **Leveling the excavated area.** Rake the excavated area to break up any clods of earth; then, with a helper, pull an 8-foot-long 2-by-4 leveling board across the area to smooth any loose dirt *(top right)*. Dampen the area with a hose, and compact the surface by pounding it with a tamper—a 2-foot square of ¾-inch plywood with a braced handle, 4 feet high, made of 2-by-4 lumber. When the surface is packed down, pull the leveling board across the area again, using it as a straightedge to make sure that the surface is reasonably even.

3 **Establishing the grade.** Mark the planned slab height *(page 60)* on the house wall, at the end of a side boundary line. Set a 2-by-2 reference stake against the wall, 2 inches outside the boundary line. Drive the stake into the ground until its top is even with the slab-height mark, then hammer a nail into the center top of the stake. Measure along the side boundary line to a point 2 inches beyond the end boundary line, and drive a second reference stake 2 inches to the side of that point, away from the slab area. Tie a string to the nail in the house stake and around the outer stake; adjust the string until it is level, using a line level set on its center point. Measure down from the string on the outer stake, to mark the planned height of the slab as adjusted for the required drainage slope *(page 60)*. Then lower the string to that mark.

Repeat for the other side of the slab. Then connect the grade marks on the outer stakes with a third string, across the end. If expansion-joint filler is needed *(page 64)*, determine where. For this 10-by-12-foot slab only one strip is necessary, midway between the side grade lines. To mark it, drive a reference stake ½ inch out from the house wall. Drive a nail into the top of the stake, as before, and stretch a string between the nail and the end grade line *(inset)*.

4 **Adding support stakes.** Tie string markers at 2-foot intervals along the grade lines. Directly below each marker, drive a 2-by-2 form-support stake deep enough into the ground so that the grade line just touches the top of the stake. When all of the support stakes are in place, mark the position of the grade lines on the corner reference stakes; then remove the lines and trim the corner reference stakes to that level, using a handsaw. Then remove all the boundary-marker strings and stakes; leave only the support stakes and the corner reference stakes.

CORNER REFERENCE STAKE

5 **Installing form boards.** Cut two 2-by-4 form boards, making each board 4 inches longer than the distance from the house wall to the corner reference stake; piece the boards if necessary. Position a board against the inside faces of the support stakes, one end butted against the house. Hold the top edge of the board level with the top of the stake nearest the house, using a block of wood as a support, and drive a sixpenny (2-inch) double-headed nail through the stake into the board; hold a small sledge against the opposite side of the board as you hammer. Nail the board to the corner stake, then to the middle stake and all the intermediate stakes.

Install a form board for the other side in the same way. Then cut a form board for the end of the slab, and nail it to its support stakes. Where this board abuts the side boards, toenail the joints with single-headed nails. Finally, for the expansion joint, cut a center board ½ inch shorter than the distance between the house and the end board. Nail the board to its support stakes on the side of the slab that will be poured first, leaving a ½-inch space at the house wall. Drive extra support stakes 6 inches on each side of any joint where two boards meet; nail the boards to the stakes, then nail a 4-by-12-inch strip of ½-inch plywood over the joint (*inset*).

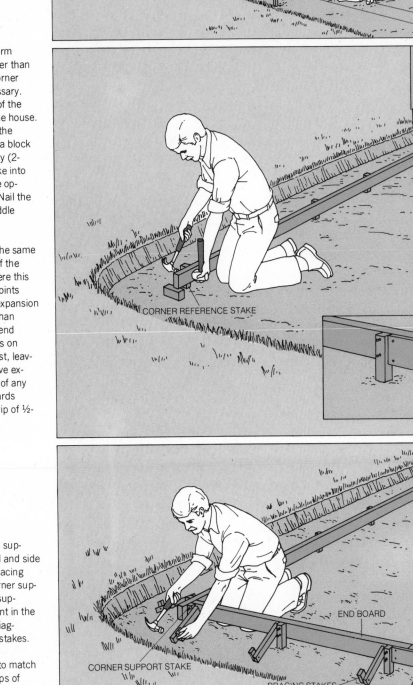

CORNER REFERENCE STAKE

6 **Bracing the form boards.** Drive an extra support stake at each corner, where the end and side boards meet. Then drive an additional bracing stake 1 foot out from each of the two corner support stakes, and from each of the other support stakes including those flanking a joint in the form. Cut 1-by-2 braces and nail them diagonally between the support and bracing stakes.

Excavate the outer part of the slab area to match the slope of the grade lines, using the tops of the form boards as a depth guide. Then smooth and tamp (*Step 2, opposite*).

CORNER SUPPORT STAKE

END BOARD

BRACING STAKES

BRACE

7 **Installing joint filler.** Lay a continuous strip of 4-inch expansion-joint filler (a flexible, asphalt-impregnated material) against the face of the expansion-joint form, and nail another strip of filler to the house wall. Begin at one corner of the form, keeping the filler level with the top of the form, and work across to the other corner, outlining any existing stairs and pushing the filler into the ½-inch gap between the house wall and the expansion-joint form. Butt the ends of the filler strip against the side forms, and fasten it to the house wall at 6-inch intervals with four-penny (1½-inch) masonry nails.

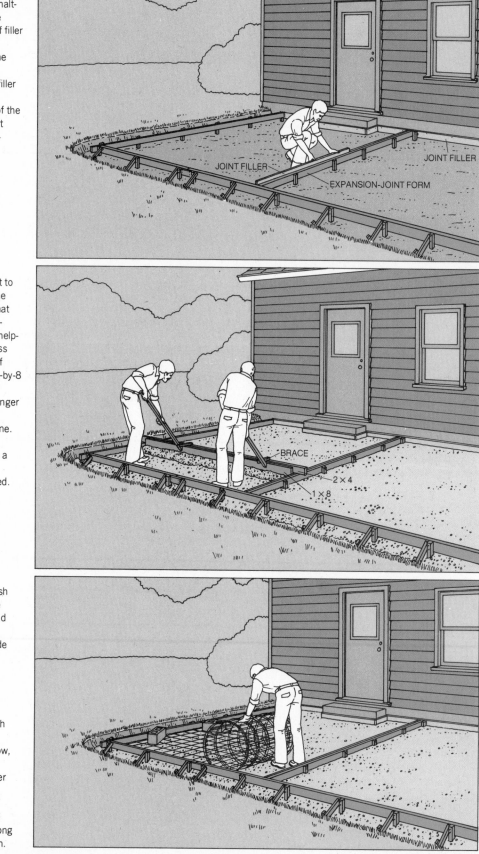

JOINT FILLER

JOINT FILLER

EXPANSION-JOINT FORM

8 **Screeding the gravel.** Pour a layer of ¾-inch gravel into each section of the slab, allowing it to spill out under the perimeter boards. Along the interior expansion joint, lift the joint filler so that the gravel will flow beneath it, bringing the filler flush with the top of the joint form. With a helper, level the gravel by dragging a screed across its surface, bringing it even with the bottom of the form boards. To make the screed, cut a 1-by-8 board 2 inches shorter than the distance between forms, and a 2-by-4 board 10 inches longer than this distance. Nail them together, with the wider board centered over the narrower one. To the face of the narrow board attach two 2-by-2 handles, each 4 feet long and tapered at a 30° angle at the bottom. Brace the handles with 2-by-2s nailed across the top of the screed.

BRACE

2 × 4

1 × 8

9 **Laying wire mesh.** Wearing gloves, unroll mesh over the gravel. Begin at the outer edge of the slab, and leave 2 inches between the mesh and the form boards. Hold the mesh down with concrete blocks. When you reach the other side of a section, anchor the mesh with more concrete blocks and, using wire cutters, cut it 2 inches short of the form board. Then turn the mesh over, and walk on it to flatten it.

Continue covering the gravel with rows of mesh until one entire section is filled, allowing an overlap of 6 inches on each row. On the last row, trim the mesh to fit around steps or other obstacles. Then tie all the pieces of mesh together with short lengths of binding wire.

Before pouring the concrete (*page 68*), lift the mesh and place bricks under it every 3 feet along the edges and down the middle of each section.

Installing Permanent Form Boards

1 **Plotting the pattern.** To divide a rectangular slab into smaller rectangular units of varied sizes, each framed permanently with wood strips, outline the slab on graph paper, with each square representing 1 square foot. Divide the scale drawing into four equal quadrants, the primary forms; then subdivide one quadrant into the desired pattern of squares and rectangles. Repeat this pattern in the other three quadrants.

Extend all the pattern lines to the perimeter of the drawing, creating a grid that will serve as a guide for the placement of strings along the form boards of the actual slab. These strings will indicate where extra form boards are needed within each quadrant for shaping the secondary forms. Plot the stake locations for these forms on the scale drawing, marking each with an X.

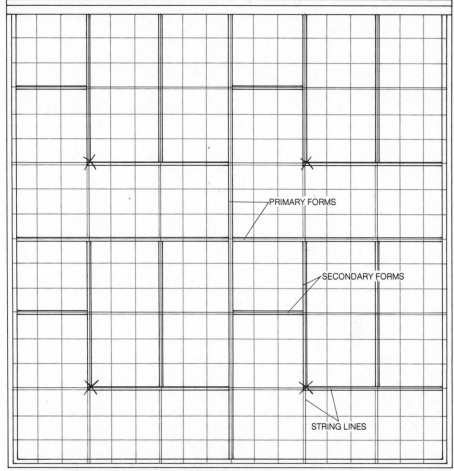

PRIMARY FORMS

SECONDARY FORMS

STRING LINES

2 **Setting up strings and stakes.** Transfer the graph-paper pattern to the slab area in two stages. First install pressure-treated boards for the primary forms; then use these to set up the string grid that will locate the position of the support stakes for the secondary forms. To install the primary forms, use the techniques shown on pages 61-64; but set the supporting stakes 1 inch lower so that they will be hidden under concrete, and nail the form boards on the outside rather than the inside of the stakes, using galvanized common nails. Position the boards so that their top edges extend 1 inch above the top of the stakes, instead of lying flush with them.

Add joint filler next to the house wall (*page 64, Step 7*), and lay a gravel bed (*page 64, Step 8*). Then install a string grid for the secondary forms, tying strings to nails driven into the house wall where necessary. Measure to make sure the strings are even with the slightly sloping bottom edges of the side form boards. Drive 2-by-4 support stakes at the marked locations, sinking them into the ground until the strings just touch their tops. With all stakes in place, mark the location of the grid strings on the primary forms; then remove the strings.

3 **Installing the secondary forms.** Cut 2-by-4 form boards to fit the dimensions of the pattern. Rest one end of a form board on its stake, covering half the stake, and toenail a tenpenny (3-inch) nail through the board into the top of the stake. Complete the corner by resting the adjoining board on the other half of the stake, toenailing it to the stake. Then nail the second board to the end of the first.

Where a secondary form board butts into the face of any other form board, drive two nails through that board into the end of the secondary board. When all the forms are in place, cut mesh to fit each section and install it (page 64, Step 9). Then drive tenpenny (3-inch) nails partway into the inside faces of the primary forms and into both faces of the secondary forms, leaving about 1½ inches of the nail exposed; the protruding ends will anchor the concrete. In driving the nails, cushion the blows by holding a small sledge against the opposite face, to keep the forms from shifting. Finally, before pouring the concrete, cover the top edges of the form boards with heavy-duty masking tape.

Building a Curved Form for a Free-form Slab

1 **Excavating the slab area.** Establish the slab shape with a garden hose, then outline it with chalk dust squirted from a squeeze bottle. Remove the hose, and excavate the area to a depth equal to the thickness of the drainage bed plus the thickness of the slab (page 60). Begin by digging a trench 1 foot outside the chalk line, then dig back and forth across the area in parallel rows. Smooth and tamp the soil in the bottom of the excavation (page 62, Step 2).

Install a string grid of grading lines above the excavation, allowing for drainage away from the house. Start the string grid by setting up rectangular boundary lines 1 foot outside the widest points on the form, squaring the corners as on page 9, Step 1. Tie intermediate grading lines at 3-foot intervals between the side lines, and between the house wall and the end line; at the house wall, tie the strings to masonry nails. Drive 2-by-2 support stakes around the slab perimeter, 1 foot in from the edge of the excavation. Space the stakes 2 feet apart along gradual curves, 1 foot apart around sharp curves. Then add support stakes for expansion joints, spacing them at 2-foot intervals. Set the tops of the stakes even with the strings (inset).

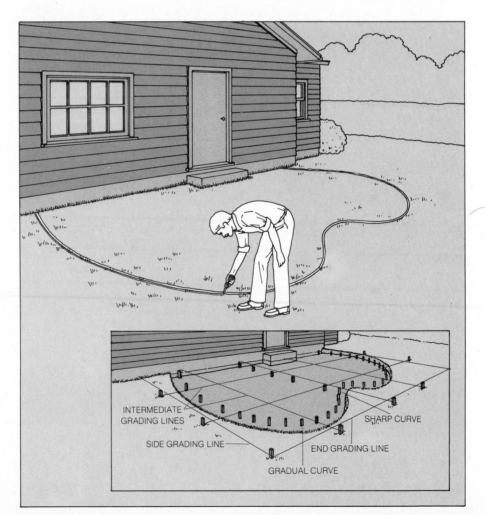

INTERMEDIATE
GRADING LINES

SHARP CURVE

SIDE GRADING LINE

END GRADING LINE

GRADUAL CURVE

2 Installing form boards. Subdivide the curves of the planned slab into sections, each one no less than 3 feet long and ending within 3 inches of a stake. Tack strips of ¼-inch lath around each section. Using the strips of lath as guides, cut form boards from ¼-inch hardboard, as wide as the planned depth of the slab. Add 3 inches, for fitting adjustments, to the two boards that butt against the house, and 6 inches to all others.

Wet each board until it bends easily and set it against its stakes, its top flush with the stake tops. Butt the first board against the house wall, and nail it to the inside of each stake with two ½-inch galvanized nails. Use a fine-toothed saw to trim the board off at the midpoint of a stake. Butt the second board against the first, and nail it to the same stake (inset). Continue until all the curved sections are in place. Add straight form boards for any expansion joints needed (page 60). Fasten expansion-joint filler against these boards, and nail additional filler to the wall of the house (page 64, Step 7).

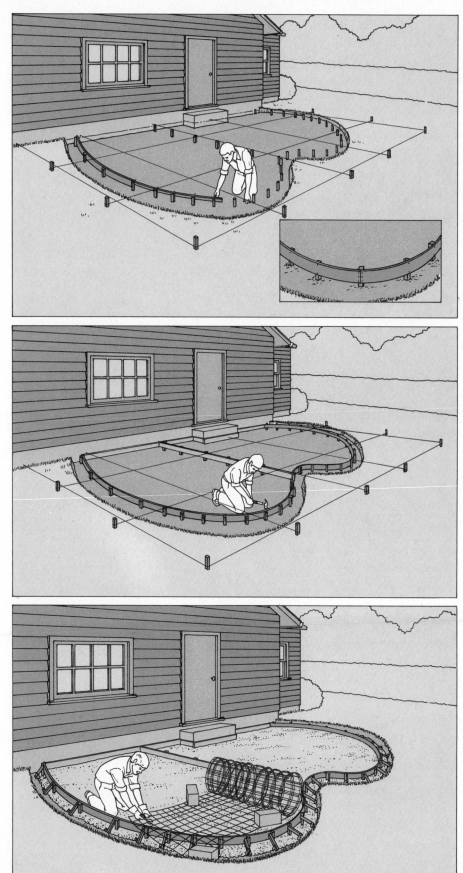

3 Adjusting the form to the grading grid. Work around the curved form, lifting or hammering down the boards and stakes until the top edge of the form just grazes the grading lines. Repeat for the straight forms of the expansion joints. When both the curved and the straight forms are adjusted, secure the support stakes with diagonal braces as on page 63, Step 6.

Correct the depth of the excavation to match the slope of the grade. Then add and screed the gravel drainage bed (page 64, Step 8).

4 Cutting mesh to fit the form. Unroll a length of wire mesh over a section of the form, allowing it to overlap the curve of the form boards where necessary. Anchor the mesh temporarily with cinder blocks. Cut the mesh along the curve, 2 inches in from the form. Remove the trimmed mesh, turn it over and roll it up in the opposite direction to flatten it. Then return it to its place. Cut additional sections of mesh, allowing each to overlap the previous section by 6 inches. Flatten the sections and tie them together with binding wire. Before pouring the concrete, place bricks every 3 feet under the mesh.

Pouring and Finishing the Paved Surface

The key requirement for pouring and finishing a concrete slab is speed. On a dry, windy day, it may take as little as three hours for freshly poured concrete to become too stiff to work. To get the job done in time, enlist the aid of several helpers. For a 10-by-12 slab, two people will need about an hour for the heavy work of pouring, leveling and floating (smoothing) the concrete, plus another two to three hours to finish the surface.

The best source of concrete for a large slab is a transit-mix company that will make up the concrete to your specifications and deliver it to the site in a ready-mix truck. When ordering the concrete, tell the supplier the exact dimensions of your slab and whether you intend to apply a pebble-aggregate surface—which requires a stiffer-than-average concrete mix—and if you wish to have it colored.

If you live in an area that is subject to freezes and thaws, make sure that an air-entraining agent—a chemical that creates tiny air bubbles in the concrete to prevent cracking—is added to the mix. For the pebble-aggregate surface shown on pages 71 and 72 buy pea gravel or other small, decorative stones from the concrete supplier: order half a ton of gravel for every 100 square feet of slab. Cross sections of redwood, such as those that

are embedded in the slab shown on pages 72 and 73, are available in 6- to 34-inch rounds at most nurseries.

Have the ready-mix truck arrive early in the morning to give you the most time to pour and finish the concrete. Avoid having the truck drive onto your property; a big mixer truck can crack sidewalks or driveways and sink into lawns. Have the truck park on the street; then lay a path of planks from the curb to the slab and transport the concrete over the planks in wheelbarrows. (If the distance from the safest parking place to the slab is more than 200 yards, haul the concrete to the site in a rented trailer equipped with a mixer. Such trailers carry up to 4½ cubic yards of concrete—enough for a 350-square-foot slab—and can be pulled onto a lawn over planks.)

If you are mixing the concrete yourself, sample the mixture to test its consistency. The concrete should be just wet enough to stick to a shovel. If it forms a dry clump, it is too stiff to work. Slowly add more water to the mixture—1 cup per cubic foot of concrete at a time—and check the consistency again.

When the concrete is ready to pour, carry about 1 cubic foot—which weighs around 150 pounds—in a wheelbarrow at a time. If you are pouring a large slab, fill

the interior forms first, running the wheelbarrows over planks laid bridgelike across the forms. So that it will be easier to remove the forms after the concrete has set, either grease the insides of the forms with motor oil or hose them down before you begin.

Once the concrete has been placed in the forms, it must be leveled, then smoothed, and its edges rounded. These steps compact the concrete and bring moisture, called bleed water, to the surface. You must wait until the bleed water has evaporated (from 20 minutes to an hour or two) before applying the finish. Use a 12-by-4-inch steel trowel to apply a smooth finish—which can be left as is, or textured to create a nonskid surface, or incised with grooves to simulate flagstones *(page 71)*.

After a slab is finished, it must be cured—kept moist and warm for at least a week to allow for the gradual chemical reactions that give concrete its full structural strength. The most common method of curing is to cover the slab with a polyethylene plastic sheet. Colored slabs and pebble-aggregate surfaces are air-cured, however—left uncovered and sprinkled several times a day with water. Wait until the slab has cured to remove the outside forms.

Filling the Forms

1 Adding the concrete. Dump enough wheelbarrowloads of concrete into the first form to fill a 3- to 4-foot-wide section across the bed, between the form boards. Then use a shovel to push the concrete into the corners of the form and to pack each successive load against the preceding one. Overfill the form by ½ inch.

After filling the section, drive a flat spade between the inner edges of the form and the concrete, to force the coarse aggregate away from the sides. Then jab the spade vertically into the concrete throughout the section, to eliminate any air pockets. If the wire reinforcement sags into the gravel base under the concrete's weight, hook it with coat hangers and pull it up so that it is embedded in the middle of the concrete.

2 **Screeding the concrete.** As each 3- to 4-foot section is filled, set a screed—a straight 2-by-4, cut 2 feet wider than the width of the form— on edge across the form boards. With the aid of a helper, lift and lower the screed in a chopping motion to force the aggregate down into the concrete. Then, starting at the top of the filled section, pull the screed across the surface of the concrete, simultaneously sliding it from side to side in a sawlike motion. Tilt the screed toward you as you pull it, so that the bottom of the board acts as a cutting edge. To level any remaining low spots or bumps, pull the screed across the concrete again, tilting it away from you. In areas around obstacles such as steps or window wells, use a short screed, cut to fit the space.

Fill and level the rest of the form in successive 3- to 4-foot sections, then move to the next form. When you cannot operate the screed from outside a form, because adjacent forms are already filled, work inside the form, wearing boots to protect your clothing from the oozing concrete.

3 **Removing the inside form boards.** After pouring and leveling all of the concrete, remove the boards supporting the expansion-joint material inside the slab. To do this, first build a bridge over the wet concrete by laying a ladder—topped with a plank and supported by concrete blocks—across the outside form boards. Pry up the interior form boards and stakes with a pry bar, then shovel concrete into the channels and stake holes. Level the fresh concrete with a short screed, then remove the bridge.

4 **Bull-floating the surface.** To compact and smooth the concrete, use a wooden bull float. First push the float forward, tilting the front edge of the blade upward, then draw it back, keeping the blade flat against the surface. Shovel fresh concrete into any remaining depressions, using a ladder bridge to reach areas beyond arm's length. Then bull-float the surface again.

5 **Edging the concrete.** When the concrete is firm enough to hold a shape, run a mason's trowel between the form boards and the outside edge of the slab, to separate the top inch of concrete from the wood *(left)*. Then push an edger back and forth along the cut *(right)*. Tilt the front of the tool slightly upward when moving it forward, and tilt the rear end upward when moving it backward. Be careful not to gouge the concrete, since any deep indentations will be difficult to fill in later finishing steps.

Wait for the bleed water on the surface of the slab to evaporate before applying the finish.

Finishing the Surface

Troweling a smooth finish. Place a pair of knee boards—1-by-2-foot pieces of ⅜-inch plywood with 2-by-2 handles nailed at the ends—on the slab. Kneeling on the boards, smooth the concrete with a hand float, holding it flat and sweeping it in overlapping arcs across the surface. Then sweep a rectangular steel trowel, held flat, across the same area. Similarly float and trowel the rest of the slab, moving the knee boards as necessary. (The concrete will be firm enough to walk on at this stage.)

After the initial floating and troweling, go back over the entire slab again with the trowel alone, this time tilting the tool slightly. Work the surface until no concrete collects on the trowel, and the blade makes a ringing sound as you move it along the surface; this means that the concrete is too hard to work any further. Run the edger between the form boards and the edges of the slab *(above, right)* to restore the edging lines.

TROWEL

FLOAT

Brooming on a skidproof surface. Hand-float and trowel the concrete (*opposite, bottom*), but eliminate the final troweling; instead, draw a damp, stiff-bristled utility brush across the surface. Either score straight lines at right angles to the forms or move the broom in arcs to produce a curved pattern. If the broom picks up small lumps of concrete, hose down the bristles to clean them; give the slab a few more minutes' drying time before you continue. If you have to press down hard to score the concrete, work fast; the concrete will soon be too hard to take a finish.

Creating a flagstone effect. Immediately after bull-floating the concrete (*page 69*), score the surface with irregularly spaced grooves ½ to ¾ inch deep, using a convex jointer or an 18-inch length of copper pipe bent into a flat S shape. Use a ladder bridge to reach inaccessible spots. After the bleed water has evaporated, hand-float and trowel the surface (*opposite, bottom*), then retool the grooves to restore the flagstone pattern to its original clarity. Brush out the grooves with a dry paintbrush to remove any remaining loose bits of concrete.

CONVEX JOINTER

A Pebble-Aggregate Surface

1 Preparing the surface. Before pouring the slab, thoroughly hose down the pebble aggregate you will embed in its surface. Then fill the forms with concrete, one section at a time as on page 68, Step 1, but pack it even with the tops of the boards rather than above them. Level the concrete with a screed notched at each end so that its bottom edge rides ½ inch below the upper edges of the form, then bull-float the surface. Use a shovel to scatter the damp pebbles evenly over the concrete. Cover the surface with a single layer of stones, using a ladder bridge, if necessary, to reach inner areas.

2 **Embedding the aggregate.** Tap the stones into the concrete with a bull float, forcing them just below the surface. After you have gone over the entire slab with the bull float, press down any stones that are still visible with a hand float, using a ladder bridge to reach the interior of the slab. Then run the hand float across the surface as on page 70, covering the stones with a thin, smooth layer of concrete.

3 **Exposing the aggregate.** After the bleed water has evaporated and the concrete is firm enough to resist indentation, brush the surface lightly with a stiff nylon broom to expose the tops of the stones. Then, while a helper sprays the slab with water, brush it again, uncovering between a quarter and a half of the stones' circumference. If you dislodge any stones, stop brushing and wait until the concrete is a bit firmer before continuing. If the concrete is difficult to wash off, work quickly to expose the aggregate before the surface becomes too stiff.

After the stones are exposed, continue to spray the surface until the water runs clear and there is no noticeable cement film left on the aggregate. Scrub individual spots missed in the general wash with a scrub brush and a pail of water. Two to four hours after exposing the aggregate, wash and lightly brush the surface again to remove any cloudy residue from the stones.

Combining Redwood with Concrete

1 **Installing redwood rounds.** Place 4-inch-thick redwood rounds directly on the gravel bed in the desired pattern. Cover the top of each round with a piece of 4-mil polyethylene, fastened with staples. Pour or shovel concrete carefully around each round. Level the concrete with a 2-by-4 screed cut short enough to fit between the rounds. Smooth the surface with a darby—a 3-foot-long board, 4 inches wide, with a short handle—instead of with a bull float. Hold the darby flat, and move it back and forth in a sawing motion to cut off bumps and fill in holes. Then run the darby over the slab a second time, sweeping it across the surface in broad arcs.

2 **Finishing the edges.** When the concrete is firm enough to hold a shape, run the pointed end of a mason's trowel around the outside of each round to cut a ¼-inch-deep, V-shaped groove. Finish the slab with a hand float and a trowel as on page 70. When the concrete has cured, remove the polyethylene covers.

Making Individual Paving Blocks

Concrete surfaces are not limited to large areas. The many individual paving blocks that make up garden pathways and edgings, or that are set in sand like the bricks on page 82 to form small patios, are merely slabs on a miniature scale. Rectangular and circular paving blocks, or pavers, are readily available at building-supply stores, but you can also make your own concrete pavers in sizes and shapes to suit your particular needs.

Pavers are generally 2½ inches thick and are poured into forms that can be made at home from 2-by-3 lumber to produce the geometric shapes shown at right, or configurations of your own design. Bottomless spring-form cake pans can be used as forms for circular pavers. You can either pour the pavers in place—setting the forms in a bed of gravel—or make them up at a separate location and position them after they have dried and cured.

Use premixed concrete—to which you need only add water—to build the pavers. Mix the concrete in a wheelbarrow, stirring it with a garden hoe. Pour the blocks on a level surface that you have covered with building paper; have the paper extend 18 inches beyond the forms on all sides to catch splashes and the overflow from screeding. Use a trowel to fill each form halfway up the sides with concrete; compact the concrete and force it into the corners with a wood block. Lay cut-to-fit sections of wire mesh over the concrete, and finish filling the forms, overfilling each one slightly. Pull a small 2-by-4 screed across the top of each form, then finish the surface with a hand float and a trowel as on page 70.

Allow the concrete to dry for a day or two, then pull off the forms. Cover the blocks with plastic or sprinkle them with water several times a day for a week to 10 days to cure them.

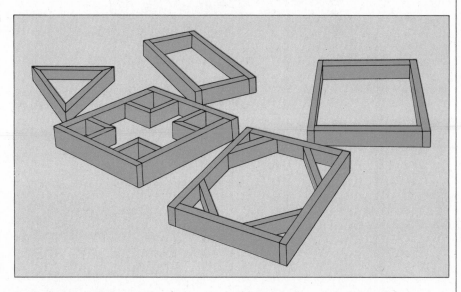

Pavers in many shapes. Forms for rectangles, octagons, crosses and triangles are made from 2-by-3 lumber joined with sixpenny nails. The octagonal and cross shapes are both built inside square frames, for extra support. Four 2-by-3s, cut the same length and mitered 45° at each end, are nailed across the corners of the frame to form an octagon. For the cross, short lengths of 2-by-3 are nailed perpendicular to the frame to form small, equal squares at each corner. The triangle is three pieces of 2-by-3 mitered 30° at each end.

Steps Designed for Flat and Sloped Sites

Steps faced with a decorative veneer of brick, stone or tile provide a handsome link between patio and house or between patio and lawn. They can be built in various ways, depending on the site or on design considerations. Some steps are solid concrete; some, on sloping sites, use the ground for support, with or without concrete bulkheads to anchor the risers. Steps may descend directly onto a patio or, where space is limited, they can approach it laterally, hugging the wall of the house. Finally, the treads can be curved instead of straight, adding an extra design element to the patio area.

Steps made of solid concrete are poured into a wooden form, in much the same way as a concrete slab. The weight of the concrete must be supported by a footing of 1¼-inch gravel that extends below the frost line, and the concrete base must extend 6 inches below ground level. Steps cut into a sloping site vary in structural needs. In mild climates, where freezing and thawing do not occur to shift the ground, steps can simply be bolstered with rock or railroad-tie risers. Otherwise, the risers are best anchored in a narrow concrete footing, with a bed of gravel beneath the treads for drainage.

Concrete steps that rise along the house wall for a distance greater than 3 feet should be tied to the foundation with reinforcing bars—round metal bars pushed into predrilled holes and set in anchoring cement. For long flights of

Making Forms for Straight and Curved Treads

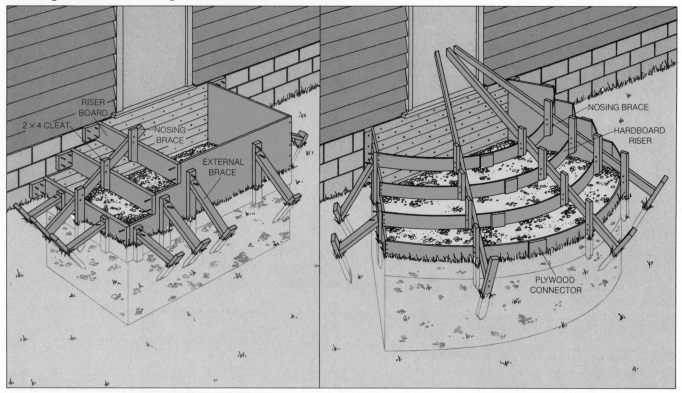

Forms for straight or curved steps. A form for concrete steps is set in a footing hole, dug deep enough to accommodate a bed of 1¼-inch gravel extending from 6 inches below ground level to several inches below the frost line. For straight steps (*left*), the form has side and back sections of ¾-inch grade D plywood and riser boards of 2-by-6 lumber. The profile of the steps is marked and cut on the side wall as on a porch-stair carriage (*pages 16-17*). The bottom riser is 6 inches deeper than the rest, to allow it to extend to the belowground footing. External bracing is provided by 2-by-4s nailed to the plywood side wall and back wall at 3-foot intervals, and at each riser as well. Additional braces shore up the bottom riser. Diagonal 2-by-4 supports are nailed to the braces and wedged against stakes driven into the ground at an angle about 18 inches out from the footing. When the steps rise against a house wall, cleats are attached to the house foundation, to provide a nailing surface for one end of the riser boards. The cleats are nailed to the foundation with double-headed nails, and double-headed nails are also used to join the riser boards to the edge of the side wall. Each riser board is held in place by cleats attached to a 2-by-4 nosing brace that is wedged against a stake. The cleats are beveled at the bottom to allow room for reaching beneath them when finishing the concrete treads. Place nosing braces at 3-foot intervals. For curved steps (*right*), riser boards are made of the same flexible ¼-inch hardboard used in forming curved slabs (*page 66*). The side walls diverge slightly to create concentric steps, necessitating riser boards of varying lengths. Determine their lengths by nailing the bottom riser in place, then bending each successive riser across the side walls while maintaining a constant distance from the previous riser. To build long spans, connect lengths of riser board by butting their ends and screwing small pieces of plywood to their outside face. Extend the nosing braces beyond the top riser; wedge them against the house wall, to hold the risers in position vertically as well as horizontally. Finally, nail ½-inch asphalt-impregnated expansion-joint filler to the house wall where the steps join it.

steps, you can save on cement by stacking cinder blocks in the wooden form to within 4 inches of the sides and top of the form. Allow for a full 4 inches of concrete over this cinder-block base, however, or the stairs will be too weak. And before adding the concrete, fill the cinder blocks with gravel and rubble.

Outdoor steps need deeper treads and shallower risers than indoor steps, for good footing and maximum visibility in all weather and all degrees of light. A minimum of 10 inches for the tread and a maximum of 7½ inches for the riser are considered safe; 4 feet is a good side-to-side width. The landing should be at least as wide as the threshold, and deep enough for an outward-swinging screen door or storm door to open fully.

Check local building codes for other requirements that may apply. Then plan the dimensions just as you would for porch steps made of wood (page 16). In calculating these dimensions, take into account the thickness of the stone, tile or brick that will cover the steps, as well as the thickness of the mortar to which the veneering materials are bonded. Also, try to base the dimensions of the steps on the size of the veneering material, in order to minimize the need for cutting.

Railings should be installed on all stairs higher than 18 inches. The sturdiest railings rest on solid-steel posts sunk into holes in the concrete and held in place with anchoring cement. Iron-railing kits, complete with posts, rails, and supporting balusters, are available at home-improvement stores. You can also order custom-made railings from an ironworks. The local dealer will take the necessary measurements and do the installation. Or have steel posts cut and drilled at an ironworks and build the sturdy steel-and-wood railings shown on page 76.

Pouring and Finishing Built-up Steps

1 Filling the form. Before pouring concrete into the form, insert reinforcing bars in the house foundation, allowing them to protrude 4 inches. Coat the inside surface of the wooden form with motor oil to prevent the concrete from sticking. Fill the form with cinder block, rubble and gravel, keeping all filler material at least 4 inches from the form. Begin filling the form by shoveling premixed concrete (page 68) into the bottom step. Use the shovel to push the concrete against the edges of the form, then fill in the center. As you work, drive the shovel into the wet concrete to break up air pockets. Level the landing and treads as for a slab (pages 68-69), and set empty beer or soda cans 3 inches into the wet concrete to make holes for the railing posts. Oil the cans to keep the concrete from sticking, and use an old screwdriver to pry them out when the concrete has set.

2 Smoothing the surface. When the concrete has set to the stage where pressing it with your thumb leaves only a slight indentation, carefully detach the riser boards and use a hand float to finish the risers. Start at the top step, and kneel on a board placed on the tread below, to distribute your weight. Finish the inside corners of the treads and their outer nosings with inside and outside step tools (inset). For a non-skid finish, sprinkle grains of aluminum oxide or silicon carbide on the landing and treads, and work them in with a metal trowel. Leave the side and back sections of the form in place for a week, and keep the concrete covered with damp burlap, to cure it. When these sections are removed, chip away small projections with a cold chisel and a ball-peen hammer, fill depressions and smooth the surface with quick-setting patching cement laid on with a mason's trowel.

75

A Custom Railing of Steel and Wood

A railing set in concrete. This railing is built with posts of 2-by-¼-inch steel bar, a corner post of 2-by-¼-inch L bar, and rails of 2-inch-thick hardwood. The posts are 39 inches long overall, allowing for 3 inches at the bottom anchored in the concrete. Holes for ½-inch bolts to fasten the handrail to the posts are drilled into each post 2 and 4 inches from the top. On the post at the front of the landing four holes are needed; the other posts need only two holes. The L bar has boltholes through both faces. Holes for guardrail bolts are drilled 19 and 21 inches from the top of the posts, two holes in the post at the front of the landing, one hole in each other post and in each face of the L bar. The posts may be set in holes cast in the concrete (*Step 1, page 75*), or may be drilled through the masonry veneer after the steps are completed. They are secured with anchoring cement.

The handrails are made of 2-by-6 hardwood, the guardrails of 2-by-4 hardwood with rounded edges, sanded smooth and coated with sealer and finish. The railings are held to the outside of the posts with ½-inch stainless-steel stove bolts, sunk in counterbored holes. At the landing corner, the railings are mitered at a 45° angle; each is bolted to one face of the L bar (*inset*). The handrail extends 2 inches past the bottom riser.

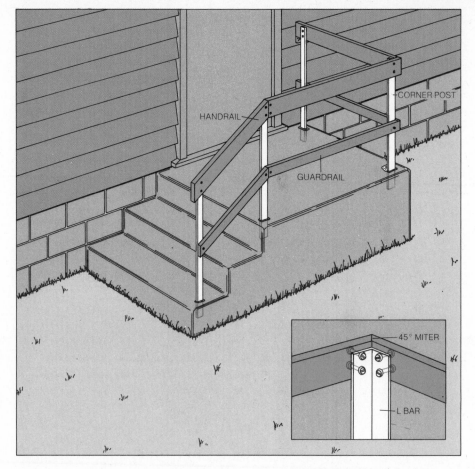

Building In-Ground Steps

1 **Finding the number and size of steps.** Drive a short stake at the top of the slope and another stake at the bottom, taller than the total height of the slope. Use a level to plumb the bottom stake, then stretch a string from the bottom of the upper stake to the top of the lower stake, using a line level to ensure that the string is level. Tie the string to the lower stake.

Find the total rise of the stairs by measuring the distance between the bottom of the lower stake and the string. Determine the total run by measuring the length of the string. Calculate the number of steps by dividing the total rise, in inches, by 6 (the ideal riser height); adjust the riser height to round off the result to a whole number. Then divide the total run by the number of steps, to find the tread depth.

With a shovel, remove the sod and any large bumps. Then tie a second string between the two stakes to establish a slope guide, and smooth the slope below the level of the string, until you have an area that is roughly the length and width of the planned steps.

2 **Excavating the steps.** Starting at the bottom of the slope and working your way up, excavate the rough treads and risers. Establish the first rough riser by cutting a 2-inch-deep trench the width of the steps. The horizontal distance from the base of the lower stake to the back of the tread should be equal to the tread depth plus the thickness of the riser material. Then cut a vertical wall at the back of the tread. Make a second rough tread by cutting horizontally into this wall at a height equal to the riser height. Make all successive risers and treads to the same dimensions. To check your work as you go along, move the slope guide along the width of the steps. If you are planning to anchor the risers in a concrete footing, it will be necessary to dig a trench 12 inches deep and 4 inches wide at the base of each riser.

3 **Setting the risers in concrete.** Mix a batch of concrete, and fill the footing trench for the bottom riser. Set the risers—bricks on end, in this example—in the concrete, flush against the rough riser and extending 2 inches higher than the rough tread above. Use a level to align the tops of the risers. Set risers in the remaining trenches in the same way. When you reach behind the top rough tread, set a row of risers to a height that will allow the tread to slope down by ¼ inch per foot to the next riser below. Allow the concrete to set for at least 24 hours.

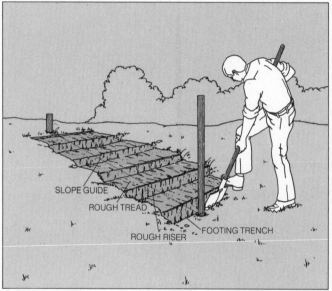

SLOPE GUIDE
ROUGH TREAD
ROUGH RISER
FOOTING TRENCH

RISER BRICKS
CONCRETE

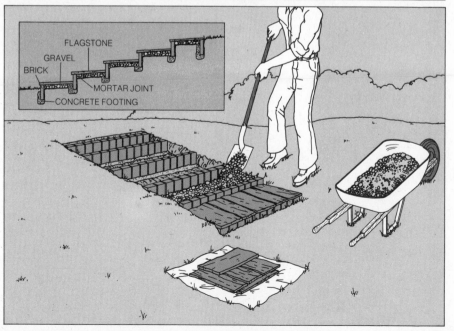

FLAGSTONE
GRAVEL
BRICK
MORTAR JOINT
CONCRETE FOOTING

4 **Finishing the steps.** Backfill the rough treads with 1-inch washed gravel to the top of the risers, and then tamp the gravel down and establish a drainage slope, ¼ inch per foot, from the back to the front of each tread. Build treads, starting at the top step, by mortaring the tread material—flagstone in this example—to the riser. Allow the tread to overlap the riser by ¾ inch, to create an overhanging nosing that makes the steps easier to see at dusk (inset).

Removing the Flaws from Existing Paving

A new veneer of brick, tile or stone can do wonders for an old concrete slab or flight of steps, turning it from an eyesore into an ornament. But before veneering can begin, the worn concrete needs some preliminary testing and may need reconditioning. First, check a slab to see if it has the proper grade for good drainage and make sure a slab or a flight of steps is structurally sound. then you may need to touch up the concrete surface to remove irregularities.

To test the soundness of concrete, drop a tire iron in several places. A sharp, ringing noise indicates that the concrete is solid; a dull thud signals crumbling beneath the surface. If crumbling has occurred, the slab or steps will have to be rebuilt. Break up the concrete with a sledge hammer or a rented jackhammer, and use the rubble as a base for a new concrete structure (page 60).

To test the grade, spray the surface with a hose. If most of the water settles in puddles or runs toward the house, the slab is badly graded. In this case, too, it is best to break up the slab and start over. Accumulated water will eventually weaken the mortar that bonds the veneer brick, tile or stone to the concrete.

Less serious surface flaws are more easily corrected. Minor cracks, small holes and large pockmarks may form with wear and age. You may also find high spots or bumps left by careless construction. Most of these flaws can be fixed with a few basic tools. Use a cold chisel and a small sledge to remove damaged concrete, a trowel and a wood float for patching. Wear goggles and gloves when concrete chips are flying.

Remove any old paint with a commercial stripper, such as methylene dichloride. Then look for high spots by drawing a metal straightedge over the surface. Any bump that protrudes ⅛ inch or more should be cut down with a mason's rubbing brick or an electric drill fitted with a silicon-carbide wheel. Both are available at building-supply stores. If you encounter an irregularity covering an area of more than 1 square foot, break up the surface with a cold chisel and fill it in as you would a large depression.

Small surface cracks, pockmarks and holes less than 1 inch deep can be filled with latex or epoxy patching mortars that are made especially for this purpose and that bond far better than ordinary patching filler. The epoxy compounds are slightly stronger and more water-resistant than the latex ones.

For larger holes or many small ones, where special compounds might be too expensive to use, chisel out the damage and trowel in an ordinary patching filler—a packaged mixture of sand and cement that comes dry; you add the water.

If you brush the damaged area with an epoxy or acrylic bonding adhesive before adding the filler, the patch will adhere more securely. Chipped corners can also be restored in this way (opposite).

When the smoothed surface is ready for veneering, remove dust and debris with a wire brush; apply a commercial concrete cleaner to remove oil, grease or other stains; and rinse with water. Then attach the bricks, tiles or stones as for a new slab (pages 80 and 88).

Making a Concrete Patch

1 Preparing the damaged area. Chip out the concrete in the damaged area with a cold chisel and a small sledge. The hole should be 1½ inches deep, the edge undercut slightly so that the bottom of the depression is wider than the top (inset). Clear away the concrete rubble with a wire brush, and spray the area with a hose. Blot up excess water with a sponge.

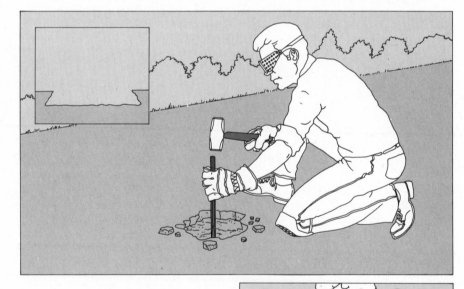

2 Adding the adhesive and filler. Spread bonding adhesive in the cavity with a stiff-bristled brush, such as one commonly used for dusting before exterior painting. Cover the area completely with an even coat, then wipe up spills around the edge of the hole with a rag. Check the manufacturer's drying-time instructions—usually about ½ hour to two hours.

Prepare the sand-and-cement filler according to the manufacturer's instructions, and trowel the mixture into the hole before the bonding adhesive loses its tackiness.

3 **Smoothing the patch.** With the patch in place, level the surface by drawing a wood float back and forth across it several times. Lift excess filler around the edges of the patch with a trowel; then, before the patch hardens, wipe the edge joint smooth with burlap or a rag.

Cover the patch with a piece of damp burlap. Keep the burlap damp for five to seven days, until the patch has cured completely.

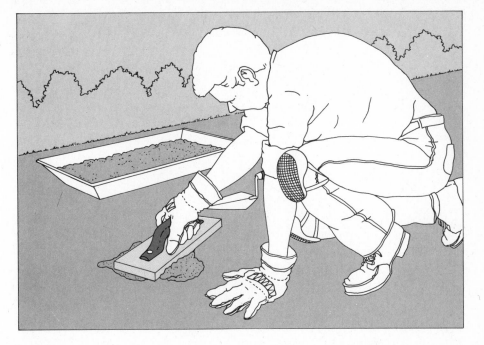

Rebuilding a Crumbling Step Corner

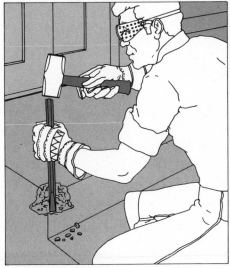

1 **Preparing the corner for a patch.** Chisel away a crumbling corner of a step until you reach solid concrete on all sides, then flatten the bottom of the cavity and undercut the sides slightly.

Measure and cut two form boards to surround the corner and contain the filler. The width of the form boards should match the height of the step riser. To steady the boards, cut two diagonal 1-by-2 braces and two 2-by-4 support stakes for each brace; the length of these stakes and their braces will depend on the height of the damaged step above the ground.

When you are ready to fill the corner, brush away any rubble and paint the cavity with a coat of bonding adhesive (*Step 2, opposite*).

2 **Filling in the corner.** While the adhesive is still tacky, coat the inside faces of the form boards with motor oil and nail them in place around the corner. Then before the adhesive hardens (follow the manufacturer's instructions, usually ½ hour to two hours), trowel the sand-and-cement patching filler (*Step 3, above*) in and tamp it down to fill the entire hole. As the patch begins to harden, level the surface with a wood float and cut away any excess filler. Cover with damp burlap; keep the burlap moist for five to seven days.

Brick Patterns to Set in Sand or Cement

Brick has been used for centuries to surface plazas, roads and walks throughout much of the world. The qualities that make it suitable for these uses make brick a good choice for a patio surface that is at once elegant and practical. A brick surface is enduring, weather-resistant and low-glare, and it is composed of small standard units that are simple to install and easy to maintain.

Durable enough to use on driveways, brick makes an attractive low-cost veneer for a concrete-slab patio. Alternatively, it can be laid without mortar, over sand, an underlayment that has certain advantages. A sand base allows rain water to seep down to tree or shrub roots, and it lets bricks move independently as the earth below settles or shifts with freezing and thawing. In addition, loose bricks can be removed in order to accommodate a broadening tree trunk or an additional flower bed.

Many bricklike blocks used today are not the traditional clay brick baked in the sun or fired in an oven, but are made of molded concrete. For this reason, the popular reddish-brown rectangular brick is only one of a wide array of colors and shapes. A variety of surface textures are also available. The best paving materials are relatively smooth, because a rough or grooved surface collects rain water; if the water freezes, the bricks may crack. But avoid bricks that are glazed or so smooth that they become slippery when wet. In a climate where the ground freezes, use bricks that are rated SW, which means they are capable of withstanding severe weather conditions.

The dimensions of paving materials also vary widely: They can be as thin as ½ inch or as thick as 3⅛ inches, and they range in length from 7½ to 11½ inches and in width from 3½ to 5½ inches. This range of sizes allows you to plan a patio with or without gaps between the bricks. For a pattern laid tight on sand—desirable for preventing weed growth—you will need special paving bricks, exactly half as wide as they are long.

Common building or face bricks are sized to accommodate a ½-inch gap for mortar—a gap that not only accentuates the pattern but serves to channel off rain water, down the long side of the brick. (To take advantage of this function, you should orient the pattern to carry water down the slope of the patio, away from the house.) For patterns set in mortar, you will also need fewer bricks—4½ bricks per square foot as against 5 bricks for patterns set tight in sand.

A sand bed should start far enough from the base of a tree for the bricks to lie level. The composition of a sand bed depends on how well the underlying soil drains. Usually a 2-inch sand base on well-tamped earth is sufficient, but you may need a 4-inch layer of washed gravel under the sand if you live in an area where rainfall is heavy or where the soil is hard-packed clay. To prevent the sand from sifting down into the gravel, cover the gravel with overlapping strips of 15-pound roofing felt or polyethylene sheeting that has been punctured with drainage holes at 4- to 6-inch intervals. If drainage is a particular problem, slope the bed about 1 inch every 4 to 6 feet. You can also lay perforated draintile or plastic tubing in the gravel layer to drain water away from wet spots.

Sand-laid bricks must be contained by a permanent edging, to check horizontal shifts. The edging is usually set at soil level, or 2 inches above the soil at the edge of a flower bed.

You can further limit shifting by filling the joints between bricks with a mixture of sand and cement, brushed in dry and then misted with water. Use a mixture of one part cement to six parts sand, and keep the patio damp for three days. To avoid staining the brick, remove all traces of cement from the surface before misting. A thin coat of silicone brick sealer, applied to the brick with a paint roller before you sweep in the cement mixture, will help prevent staining.

Weeds may grow in the sand bed if the bricks are not laid tight. A vapor barrier of perforated roofing felt or plastic sheeting directly below the bricks will control most weeds, but herbicides or weeding may be needed to rid cracks of all unwanted plants. Be careful not to use weed killers close to trees and other desirable plants.

The moss that sometimes grows between bricks in shady areas can be attractive, but on the patio surface it can be a slippery hazard; if necessary, you can remove it with ammonium sulfamate, sold at garden-supply stores. In damp areas, bricks sometimes are discolored by mildew; you can remove it by scrubbing the bricks with household bleach.

If weeds are a problem—or if a stronger, more permanent patio is wanted—bricks can be set in mortar on a concrete slab. Prepare the slab as shown on pages 60-67, to ensure a good bond between brick and concrete. The best mortar for outdoor use—type M—is available in ready-mixed form from masonry and building suppliers. Using a hoe, mix the mortar in a wheelbarrow according to the package instructions; add more water if necessary as you work, to keep the mortar just soft enough to slide easily off the hoe. Dampen the bricks thoroughly before applying mortar, and use leather-palmed work gloves to protect your hands from irritants in the mortar.

You will not need an edging for mortared brick, but you may want to add one to protect and hide the edges of the concrete slab. Set such a border before surfacing the slab, so that the border will serve as a reference level for the surface bricks. If the slab has expansion joints, matching joints are required in the brick veneer. Fill the expansion joint between bricks with polyethylene rope, then cover the rope with self-leveling polysulfide or silicone caulk.

Brick used for paving. Of the thousands of sizes, shapes and shades available in bricks and bricklike blocks, those used for paving fall into three categories: common or building brick, face brick and interlocking concrete pavers. Common or building brick (top) is ordinary clay brick, whose color varies with the natural color of clay in an area. Dimensions are about 2¼ by 3⅝ inches—to accommodate mortar joints. Face brick, more durable and expensive than common brick, includes bricks called pavers (middle), with widths exactly half their lengths, to fit mortarless patterns. Interlocking pavers (bottom), long used in Europe and usually made of concrete, are defined by their shape. When pavers are combined in a pattern, each one locks its neighbor into place, preventing shifting.

Primary paving patterns. These four patterns can be used as shown, or in combination to give varied surface designs. Bricks laid in rows for a jack-on-jack pattern (top) are difficult to align over a large area, but a double row of jack-on-jack pattern is often used to frame another pattern. In a variation, running bond (below), the bricks are staggered. It is an easy all-purpose pattern, laid with or without mortar. Two locking patterns, herringbone (middle) and basket-weave (bottom), increase the durability of a mortarless patio; each brick is held in place by a brick perpendicular to it. Herringbone can be laid diagonally, to direct a viewer's eye in a certain direction. To vary basket-weave, shown here with brick faces exposed, set the bricks on their sides, three to a square, for a tighter pattern.

Two designs for added drama. A circular patio (top) around a tree, statue or fountain emphasizes the object you wish to feature. Beginning with two circles of half bricks, the pattern radiates outward to fill an area of any shape.

The scalloped pattern (bottom), often used on European boulevards, adds a graceful touch to a patio. Rows of bricked arcs enclose scalloped spaces loosely filled with whole and half bricks.

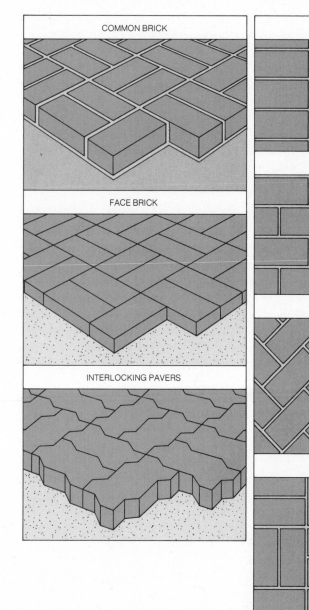

COMMON BRICK

FACE BRICK

INTERLOCKING PAVERS

JACK-ON-JACK

RUNNING-BOND

HERRINGBONE

BASKET-WEAVE

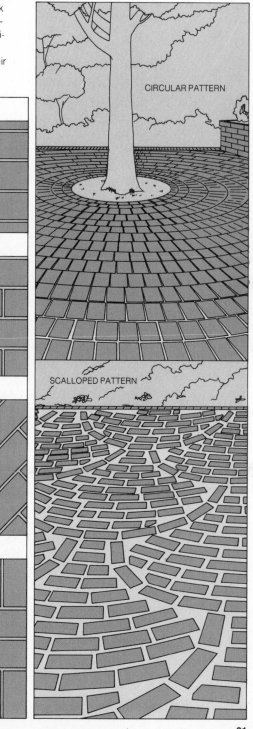

CIRCULAR PATTERN

SCALLOPED PATTERN

Laying Bricks on a Bed of Sand

Setting edging brick. Establish the edges of the patio with stakes and string *(page 61)*, then dig a bed for the bricks and sand—with a deeper trench around the perimeter for upright edging bricks. To avoid unnecessary brick cutting, first do a test run with edging brick and a row of facing brick, adjusting the perimeter to incorporate as many whole bricks as possible. Remove the test bricks, and dig deep enough to accommodate the surface bricks and the sand or the sand-and-gravel base required *(page 62)*, with a drainage slope of ⅛ to ¼ inch per foot away from any wall. Then, using a square-edged spade, dig a trench about 2¼ inches wide and 4½ inches below the original soil level, just inside the edges of the bed. Set bricks upright in the trench, and tamp earth against them to hold them vertical, the top edges touching the string guide. For a flower-bed border, let the edging extend 2 inches above where the paved surface will be. Use the reference strings to align the border bricks with each other as well. To make a saw-tooth pattern with teeth protruding 2 inches above the surface *(inset, left)*, set the bricks at an angle of 45° in the trench. Other choices for edgings include rot-resistant redwood 2-by-6s *(inset, center)*, set in a narrower trench, or upright bricks set in a curve *(inset, right)* for a rounded corner. To lay out a curved corner, use a level to align the tops of the bricks. Flatten the earth inside the bed with a tamper *(page 62)*, add washed gravel and a vapor barrier if necessary, then spread a 2-inch layer of sand over the bed. Rest a screed on the edging bricks *(page 62)* to smooth the sand; dampen the sand, then tamp the surface thoroughly again.

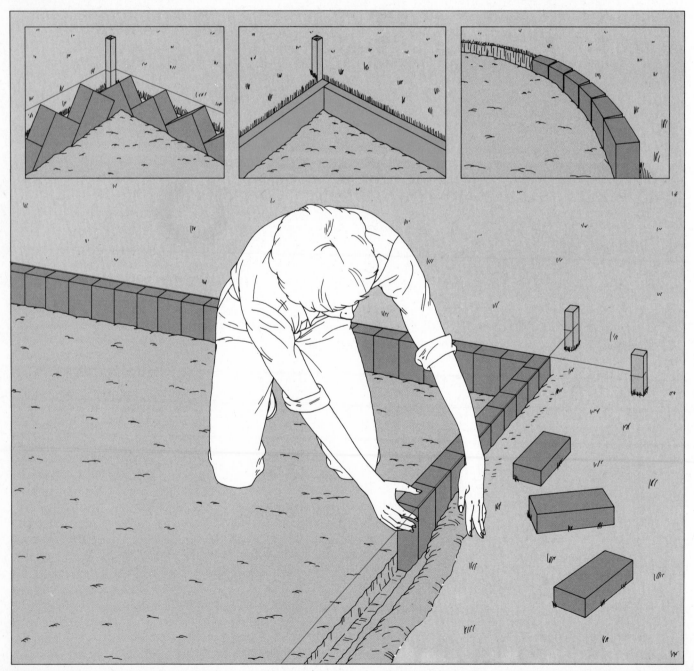

EDGING

SAND

HALF BRICK.

RUBBER MALLET

TORPEDO LEVEL

BRICKSET

SLEDGE HAMMER

A Circular Patio to Surround a Tree

1 **Starting with brick circles.** After excavating and edging the area to be paved around a tree, tamp a 3-inch level bed of damp sand in place, then set a circle of half bricks around the tree. To establish a guideline for this circle, loop a garden hose around the tree trunk, and measure out from it to scribe a circle. This circle need not be geometrically accurate—the bricks themselves will tend to correct slight irregularities. But it should be a minimum of 3 feet in diameter, to avoid wide gaps between the outer corners of the half bricks. Tap the half bricks into place with a rubber mallet, wedging the inner corners tight against each other. Lay a second course against the first; cut the last half brick in each row, if necessary, to achieve a tight fit.

2 **Setting the whole bricks.** Set concentric circles of whole bricks in the sand bed so that their inner edges touch at the corners and butt against the preceding row. As you tap each brick into place with the rubber mallet, use a 4-foot mason's level to align the brick; add or remove sand under it if necessary. The patio should be perfectly level, so that rain water is neither drained away from the roots nor pooled around the trunk. Continue building concentric circles out to the edging; then, if necessary, build concentric arcs to fill the rest of the area.

3 **Filling gaps at the edge.** For each gap near the edging strip that is smaller than a whole brick, measure and cut a brick section to fit tightly; use a 4-pound sledge hammer and a brickset, as shown on page 84. Use a rubber mallet to drive the brick into place. You can ensure a tight fit by holding the brick over the gap and drawing the cutting line with a wax pencil, then cutting the piece a bit larger. Chip away any extra brick with the sharp end of a mason's hammer. Use a stiff-bristled brush to distribute sand evenly over the surface. Then gently sweep diagonally across the bricks with a soft-bristled dust brush. Sprinkle the surface with a hose, to settle the sand further. You may have to repeat the procedure to fill the cracks entirely.

A Choice of Methods for Cutting Bricks

Using a brickset or saw. To cut a small number of bricks, use a wide chisel—called a brickset—and a small sledge hammer with a 4-pound head (*left*); to cut many bricks, score them with a circular saw equipped with a carbide masonry blade (*right*), and use a mason's hammer to break them. If you are using a brickset, cushion the brick on sand or a board, and score it along the cutting line. Hold the brickset upright with the beveled edge facing away from you, and strike the tool sharply with the sledge. Tilt the brickset slightly toward you and strike again, thus breaking the brick. To do the scoring with a circular saw, hold the brick in a simple jig made of 2-by-4 scraps, spaced a brick's width apart and nailed to a piece of plywood. Set the saw for a ¼-inch cut and slowly guide the blade along the cutting line, grooving the brick. Turn the brick over and make a matching groove on the other side. Then remove the brick, and tap the unwanted portion with a mason's hammer (*inset*) to break it off. Wear gloves and goggles whenever you cut brick. Practice on a few broken bricks before you cut the bricks you will use.

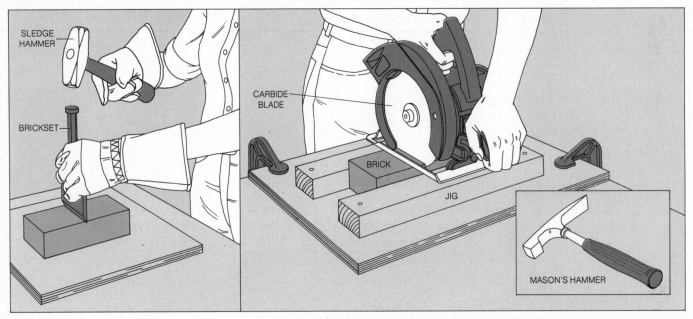

SLEDGE HAMMER

BRICKSET

CARBIDE BLADE

BRICK

JIG

MASON'S HAMMER

Laying a Herringbone Patio

Using a string guide. Starting on one edge of the patio, begin setting rows of bricks in the bed of sand, using a string stretched across the patio edging to line up each row. Establish the reference line for the first row by setting a brick in each corner at a 45° angle to the edging, tapping it into the sand with a rubber mallet until it is flush with the edging bricks. Then stretch the string between two other bricks, set just outside the edging, so that the string passes over the inner edges or corners of the two bricks just laid. As you set the remaining bricks in the first row, line them up with the string, and add or remove sand to adjust the level of each brick. When you reach the end of a row, wedge bricks of the next row into the Vs formed by bricks of the preceding row, starting with the end bricks and using them as guides for the string.

Repeat for each row, leaving gaps at the ends where whole bricks will not fit. When you have filled the area with whole bricks, fill the gaps with brick pieces that you have cut to fit (*above*). Then sweep sand into the cracks.

Setting Bricks in Overlapping Scallops

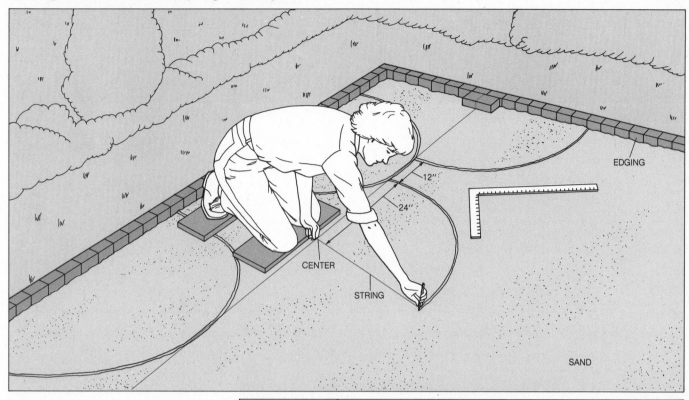

1 **Scribing scallop arcs.** On an edged sand bed, stretch a string between two bricks to establish a base line for scribing semicircles with a string-and-nail compass. Give each arc a radius of 24 inches, locating the centers 60 inches apart so that there is a 12-inch space between arcs.

After scribing arcs across one end of the patio area, with partial arcs at the sides if necessary, move the string so that it stretches across the tops of the arcs. Scribe another row of arcs, positioned with their centers at the halfway points between the arcs in the first row; use a 24-inch carpenter's square to locate each new center. Kneel on boards, to avoid disturbing the arcs you have already scribed. Continue scribing arcs until you have filled the area, using partial arcs at the far edge if necessary.

2 **Filling the scallops.** Line the outside of each scribed arc with whole bricks, using about 10 bricks for each arc in the first row and nine bricks for each arc in the succeeding rows. Then, starting in the space between arcs, place a half brick at the bottom edge, a three-quarter brick above it, and 25 to 32 whole bricks in slightly curving rows to fill each scallop *(inset)*. Fill the partial arcs with whole bricks and any large gaps with cut bricks. Sweep sand into the cracks.

A Brick Veneer
for a Concrete Slab

1 **Setting brick in mortar.** To prepare for laying brick atop a concrete slab, position a string one brick's width from the edge of the slab and ½ inch higher than the thickness of a brick. Moisten the slab; then set the bricks in ½ inch of mortar, with ½-inch gaps between bricks. If you have put edging brick around the face of the slab, leave a ½-inch gap between the surface bricks and the edging as well.

Use a large mason's trowel to spread, or butter, about ½ inch of mortar on the rough face of each brick; then make a shallow groove down the center with the point of the trowel. Turn the brick over, and set it in place on the slab, using a piece of ½-inch plywood as a spacer to keep the gaps uniform. Tamp the brick firmly with the trowel handle until the top of the brick is even with the string. Lay successive rows until the surface is covered with whole bricks, then go back and fill in any gaps with cut bricks. Allow the mortar to dry at least 24 hours before walking on the surface.

For small jobs—12 square feet or less—you can set bricks on a mortar bed spread on the moistened slab. Lay ½ inch of mortar, smooth it with a screed and score it with a notched rectangular trowel. Set the bricks on the mortar, and tamp them lightly into place with the trowel.

2 **Filling gaps with mortar.** After you allow the mortar to dry for at least 24 hours, use a grout bag with a ½-inch nozzle to fill the gaps. Mix type M mortar until it has the consistency of a thick milkshake. To eliminate lumps, sift the dry mortar through a scrap of window screen before mixing it with water. Fill the grout bag, and roll the end of the bag to extrude mortar through the nozzle and into the gaps. Pack the mortar into the gaps with a ½-inch joint filler, adding more mortar if necessary to fill them to the top. Smooth and level the joints with a trowel.

About one hour later, clean away ragged bits of mortar with the trowel. Three hours later, smooth the joints with a stiff brush or a wad of burlap, and hose the patio clean. Let the mortar cure for several days before attempting to remove any mortar stains; use muriatic acid.

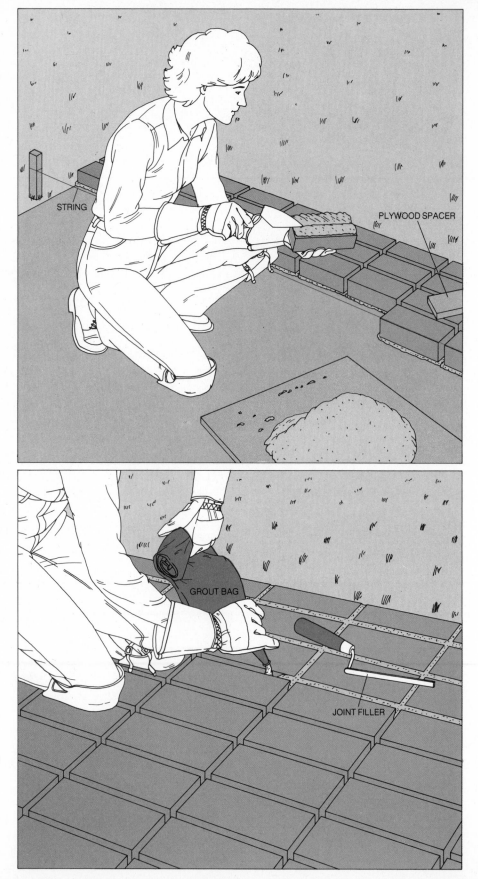

STRING

PLYWOOD SPACER

GROUT BAG

JOINT FILLER

Covering Steps with Bricks

By combining special tread bricks with ordinary bricks, you can veneer concrete stairs to match a brick patio in color and pattern. The tread bricks, with rounded nosings, are made in sizes to provide a slight overhang at the front of each step, increasing safety by creating shadows that make the steps easier to see at dusk.

These tread bricks are available in two sizes: the same length and width as the regular paving bricks, and a larger size, twice the width and one and one-half times the length of regular bricks, to fit the average 12-inch-deep stair tread.

If you build a form and pour the concrete core yourself (pages 74-75), design it to fit the bricks you plan to use. To veneer existing steps, choose bricks with dimensions that will cover the core with a minimum of cutting. In particular, choose a brick width that will allow you to cover risers with whole bricks.

No matter how thin a veneer you put over existing concrete steps, the bottom riser will be higher than the rest. To compensate, you can build a walk leading to the steps. If you start from scratch, make the first step shallower than the others by the thickness of a tread brick.

In either case, you will need to add a footing of poured concrete 4 inches wide and 1 foot deep around the step core, to support the brick veneer on the sides and the first riser.

The best mortar mix for step veneering is type M, formulated for exterior use. Mix about 1 cubic foot at a time, enough to set 25 to 30 bricks. Dampen both concrete and bricks before mortaring, to ensure proper adhesion. Expansion joints are needed where a stair landing meets a door threshold, and where a brick patio or walk meets the sides or front of the brick veneer.

1 Encasing the step sides. To start the first course of bricks on one side of the stairs, use a half brick, mortared to the footing. Set it so that it projects beyond the bottom riser by the width of one brick and a mortar joint. Complete the first course by mortaring bricks to the footing and the concrete core, using a mason's level to align them with the first half brick. Lay another course on top of the first, starting with a whole brick. Continue until the brick casing is even with the tread; then start casing the next step as you did the first, with a protruding half brick. Continue to the landing, then veneer the other side of the steps.

2 Laying the tread bricks. Mortar bricks to the front of the bottom riser, bringing them to the level of the first tread. To cover the tread, begin at one corner with a starter brick, which has two adjoining rounded edges, setting it in mortar so that its nosing protrudes about 1 inch at the front and side. Set another starter brick at the other end of the tread. Fill the rest of the tread with stretcher bricks, spacing them evenly between the starters and adjusting the width of mortar joints if necessary. Use a mason's level across the tread to align these bricks. Fill the gap between the tread bricks and the front of the next riser with regular bricks. Cover each tread and riser in this way, then pave the landing with bricks.

The Many Pattern Possibilities of Tile

Hard-fired clay tiles, set in mortar over concrete, form a paving of exceptional beauty and durability. Commonly called patio tiles, they are usually unglazed and come in a variety of types; quarry, paver and mosaic tiles are the most familiar.

Quarry tiles are recognizable by their smooth surface and right-angle edges, and are widely available in squares, rectangles, hexagons and octagons. Paver tiles are somewhat irregular in size, with a textured surface and rough or rounded edges; they are thicker than quarry tiles and are most often found in squares and hexagons. Mosaic tiles, individual tiles already spaced and mounted on a 1- or 2-foot-square mesh backing or paper covering, make fast work of intricate designs, but are seldom unglazed; for outdoor use, look for a mat finish, which will not be slippery when wet. Any outdoor tile must be frostproof; buy tile with an absorption rate of 6 per cent or less.

To estimate the number of tiles needed for a particular project, multiply the length of the area by the width—use the longest measurements across a free-form slab. Then add 5 to 10 per cent extra, for waste. Remember that the width of the mortar joints will affect your calculations. For example, a 10-by-10-foot patio will require only 96 square feet of 6-by-6 tiles when set with ⅛-inch mortar joints.

Patio tiles last longer and require less maintenance when set in a mortar made with a latex tile-setting liquid, available from cement and tile dealers. For small jobs use a ready-mix mortar, adding the latex in place of water. For bigger jobs, make a mortar by mixing 3 cups each of portland cement and fine masonry sand into 2 cups of the latex. Apply the mortar with a trowel that has ¼-inch notches; one batch will cover 6 square feet.

Mortar joints between ceramic tiles are stronger and more flexible when they are filled with grout that is also mixed with the latex tile-setting liquid instead of water. Ceramic-tile grout comes premixed in a variety of shades in 5- and 10-pound bags; a 5-pound bag will fill the joints of 5 square feet of paver or quarry tile, or 10 square feet of mosaic tile. You can also make your own grout by mixing equal parts of portland cement and fine masonry sand with sufficient latex liquid to make a thick paste.

Before setting the tile, take time to examine the concrete slab for flaws. Repair cracks, fill holes and smooth out any bumps that are more than ⅛ inch high (page 78). Note the position of expansion joints, if any, between sections of slab; try to build your tile pattern around them. For all patterns except those made with tiles of random shapes (opposite, bottom), do a dry run of the tile placement. Space the tiles precisely and mark those that need to be cut to fit curving or out-of-square edges. Adjusting the mortar-joint width can sometimes eliminate the need to cut edge tiles.

If a great many tiles need to be cut, it may be simpler to take them to a dealer.

Otherwise, cut them yourself. For tiles more than ½ inch thick, you will need a circular saw fitted with a silicon-carbide masonry blade, but tiles less than ½ inch thick are most easily and cheaply cut with a senior cutter (page 91), which you can rent from a tile dealer. Be sure to buy extra scoring wheels to use as replacements when the original wheel becomes dull. For long shallow curves a microcutter is ideal, though you can also use tile nippers to chip away curves piece by piece (page 91).

When the dry run is complete, pick up the tiles in their order of placement and set them aside. If the layout is very complex, numbering the back of the tiles will help in restoring this sequence. Then dampen the slab, trowel the mortar on, and set the tiles as described on the following pages. Work in small sections; tiles must be laid while the mortar is still soft. If the area is very large, you can break up the job into manageable sections and lay the tiles over the course of several days.

Allow the mortar to cure for a full 24 hours before the joints are grouted, but then do the grouting within the next 24 hours—otherwise, the grout may not bond to the mortar. To prevent tiles and grout from becoming stained, you can seal the finished paving with a 5 per cent silicone solution. Or you may prefer to use a small brush to seal only the grout, which usually is lighter than the tile and thus shows stains more readily.

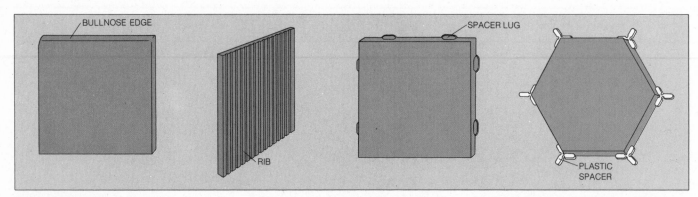

Aids to tile installation. Unglazed paver and quarry tiles are available with a number of features designed to make their installation easier and to accommodate them to special situations. Bullnose tiles are rounded on either one edge or two—for edges, corners or step caps. Ribbed tiles are scored on the back in parallel ridges, to improve the bond between the mortar and tile. Spacer lugs, molded into the tile edge, help you get even joints between tiles almost automatically. Serving the same purpose, for tiles that are stamped rather than molded, are plastic spacer lugs, which are fitted against the corners of each tile as it is laid and are left in place to be covered over later with grout.

Composing Patterns with Shaped Tiles

Repeating a single shape. Paving patterns formed from tiles of a single shape can be remarkably varied. Here, with 1 square foot outlined, they range from a simple stacked pattern made by lining up square or rectangular tiles (*below,*

left) to the complex honeycomb that practically forms itself when interlocking hexagon or octagon tiles are butted together (*below, center*). With mosaic tiles mounted on flexible backing in 12-inch squares, the pattern possibilities are

endless, for the tiles not only are varied in shape and color, but also are available in preassembled modular designs that can be put together to form border patterns or allover repeats of flowers or geometric designs (*below, right*).

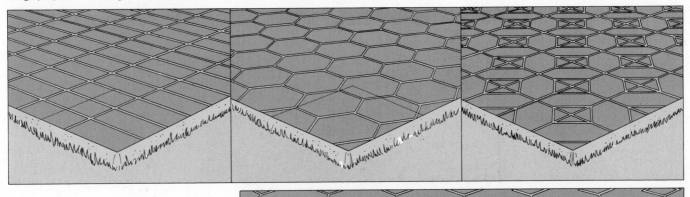

Repeating two shapes. By alternating two tile shapes, you can achieve an intricate pattern that is no more difficult to lay than a single-shape design. The traditional octagon-and-dot pattern (*top right*) builds automatically with the laying of the first 8-inch octagon, which establishes the placement for all the other octagons and for the intervening 3-inch squares, or dots. The square-and-picket pattern (*right*), which mimics a design commonly found in wood parquet floors, builds from an 8-inch square surrounded by four 3-by-11-inch pickets. Together they form the lozenge that becomes the basic unit of the overall tile design.

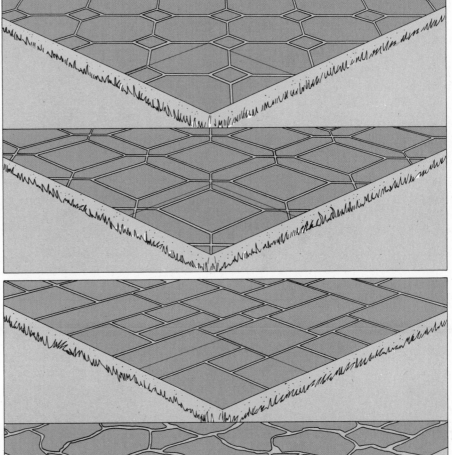

Random patterns from multiple shapes. Rectangular and square slate-colored tiles in a variety of sizes appear to be set at random to create a mingled pattern (*right*), but in fact there is a definite order to the design. Tiles for this kind of pattern are sold by the square foot, although there are a number of ways of placing the tiles within each square-foot unit.

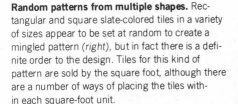

Truly random in design is the rubble pattern (*bottom right*), whose components are simply broken paver tiles with their edges smoothed. These too are available by the square foot; designs can be made by outlining sections with a continuous mortar joint.

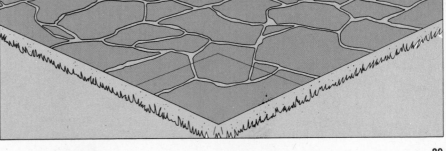

Starting the Tile Sequence

Rectangular slabs. Begin either at a corner away from the house or at an expansion joint. Work toward a far corner (*near right, Arrow 1*), and trim the last tile to fit.

If the tiles are interlocking hexagons or octagons, set tiles along the remaining part of this first row; begin on the opposite side of the expansion joint (*Arrow 2*), again trimming the corner tile if necessary. Using the last full tile nearest the far corner as a guide, set a row of tiles perpendicular to the first, along one edge of the slab (*Arrow 3*). Alternate tiles may have to be cut. Set succeeding rows (*Arrows 4 and 5*) in the same manner until the entire slab is covered. With hexagonal or octagonal tiles, some tiles must bridge the expansion joint. Finally, cut tiles to fill in the gaps remaining around the edge.

For square or rectangular tiles in a simple stack pattern, set the first row as above, beginning at an expansion joint and working out to a far corner. At the corner use the last full tile as the apex of a pyramid, and set tiles in the numbered sequence illustrated (*far right*). Work in diagonal rows until the slab is covered. Then cut tiles to fill any gaps left around the edges.

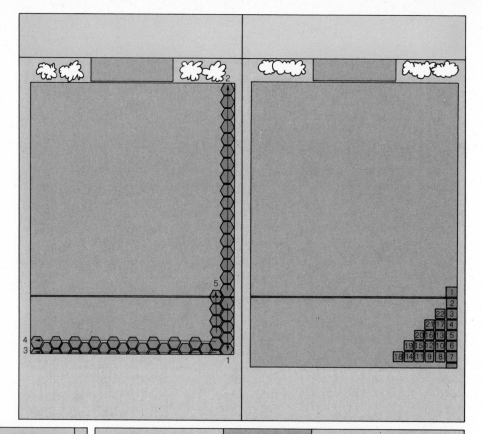

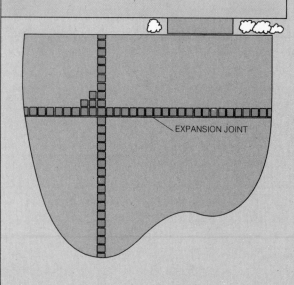

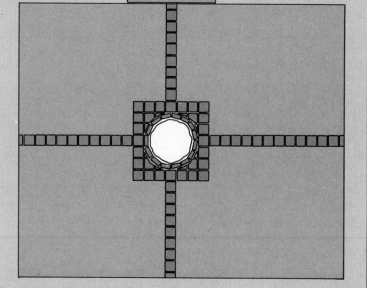

Free-form slabs. If a slab has irregular or curving edges, divide it into quadrants by snapping perpendicular chalk lines across its widest dimensions. Or use intersecting expansion joints to establish these quadrants. Fill each quadrant with tile, beginning at the intersecting guidelines and working out to the edges as in the pyramid sequence used in laying the stack pattern (*above, right*). Trim tiles to fit as necessary.

Interrupted slabs. If a slab is interrupted by an obstacle such as a tree or pool, square off the obstacle with tiles and then fill in the square with additional tiles, trimmed as necessary to fit around the obstacle. Add an edge of border tiles, if desired. Then divide the slab into quadrants, using a tile at the midpoint of each side of the square as a reference point. Lay rows of tiles along the quadrant lines, and fill in each quadrant with parallel rows of tiles. Cut the outer tile in each row to fit the edge of the slab.

Three Techniques for Cutting Tiles

Using a senior cutter. Draw a pencil line across the tile where the cut is to be made, and position the tile on the cutter plate, pencil line directly beneath the scoring wheel. Set the adjustable fence to hold the tile in place. Slide the cutter handle toward you along the bar, then tilt the handle forward until the tiny scoring wheel rests on the pencil line. Push the handle forward, scoring the tile in one continuous motion. Then lift the cutter handle and pull it back to the midpoint of the tile. Lower the handle and tap it sharply with the side of your hand, so that the tile snaps into two pieces.

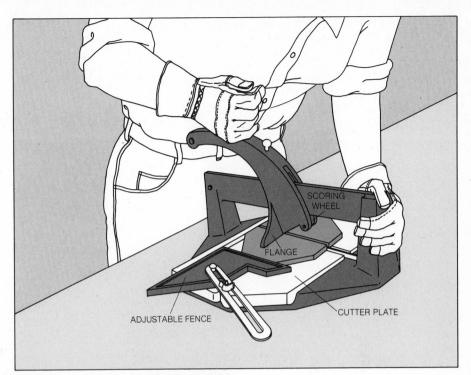

SCORING WHEEL

FLANGE

ADJUSTABLE FENCE

CUTTER PLATE

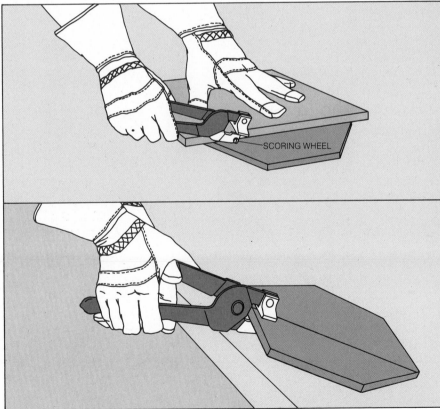

SCORING WHEEL

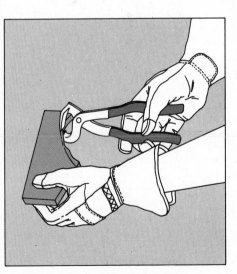

Using a microcutter. Align a straightedge with the pencil line you have made on the tile to indicate the cut. Run the scoring wheel across the tile in one continuous motion; press firmly to avoid having to make a second run, which would increase the chance of a ragged break. Grasp the tile between the jaws of the cutter, aligning the jaws with the center of the scored line, and squeeze the cutter handles. For tiles that are ribbed on the back, the scored line should run at right angles to the ribbing.

To cut a shallow curve with a microcutter, score a freehand line with the scoring wheel.

Cutting with tile nippers. Grasping the tile firmly in one hand, use the nippers to chip off small pieces of tile. Work in from the edge toward the pencil line indicating the desired shape, and hold the nippers so that the jaws are at an angle to the section of line you are approaching. When the rough cut is complete, smooth the edges with a piece of brick or a small stone.

Laying the Tiles in Mortar

1 **Applying the mortar bed.** Using the appropriate tile-setting pattern as a guide *(page 90)*, dampen an area of about 6 square feet; for example, if you are setting the first tiles in a line, the dampened area would be a long, narrow rectangle. Apply a ¼-inch-thick layer of mortar over a small section of the dampened area—about 1 by 3 feet. Use the smooth edge of a rectangular notched-blade trowel to scoop up and spread the mortar; then turn the trowel and draw the notched edge through the mortar, leaving a pattern of uniform ridges. Keep a pointing trowel near for scraping dripped mortar from the slab. Rinse both trowels often in a bucket of water, to remove mortar before it dries.

2 **Laying the tiles.** Following the tile-setting pattern established, set the first tile in the pattern sequence. Hold the tile by its edges and lower it onto the mortar bed, forcing the mortar against the back of the tile. Set plastic spacers against the corners, and add a second tile. Continue laying full tiles across the mortar bed, then add cut tiles as needed at the edge. Tap the tiles with a rubber mallet to embed them, checking the tiled surface every four or five tiles for levelness. Continue until the entire slab is filled.

When you are laying interlocking tiles over an expansion joint, be sure to leave a ⅜-inch space between the edges of the tiles that lie nearest the joint. A good way to mark this space is to set 2-inch lengths of ⅜-inch dowel between the tiles at 6-inch intervals *(inset)*.

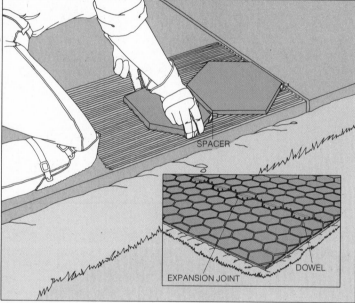

Finishing the Surface

1 **Grouting the joints.** After allowing the mortar to cure for 24 hours, place small mounds of grout at intervals along the mortar joints over an area 3 or 4 feet square, and use a dampened float to spread the grout over the tiles. During this operation, kneel on a piece of plywood to distribute your weight and avoid displacing the tiles. Moisten the float from time to time by dipping it in a bucket of water.

When grouting an area near an expansion joint, stuff the joint with rolled newspaper to keep it free of grout. This will entail removing the dowels that demarcate the expansion joint.

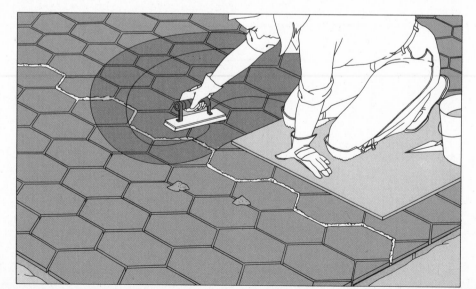

2 **Cleaning the tiles.** Let the grouted joints dry for 10 minutes, then remove excess grout from the tiles by sweeping a damp sponge across them in a circular motion. Rinse the sponge often in clean water, but keep it barely moist, to avoid saturating the grout. Excess water will wash the pigment out of colored grout.

When all the joints are filled, cover the edge of the slab with a finishing coat of grout, if desired (*page 94*). Mist the tiled surface every four hours for the first day, to let the grout cure slowly. After two more days, remove the lime haze from the tile surface by buffing with a dry cloth.

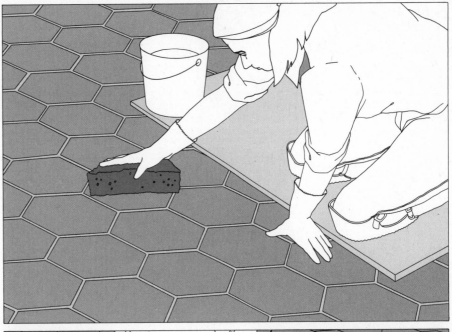

3 **Filling the expansion joint.** After the grout is cured, remove the rolled newspaper from the expansion joint and press lengths of ⅜-inch polyethylene-foam rope into the crevice (*right*). Caulk over the foam rope with a silicone or polysulfide caulk (*bottom right*), wiping away the excess caulk immediately with the solvent recommended by the manufacturer. Allow the caulk to dry before walking on the tiles.

If you are sealing the tiles, brush two coats of sealer over the tiled surface, or over the joints alone. Be sure that the tilework is completely dry before applying the sealer.

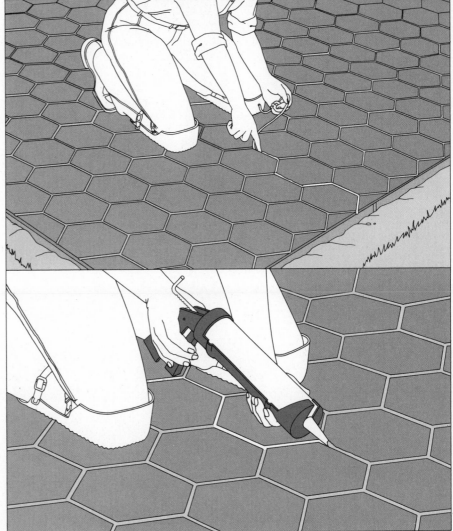

A Finished Edge
for a Tiled Slab

Trimming with grout. Using a pointing trowel, apply grout to the exposed edge of the slab. Taper the grout into a wedge shape by holding the trowel at a 45° angle to the face of the tiles. Keep the grout damp for the first day of curing by sprinkling it with water every four hours; then allow it to cure an additional three days. Seal as on page 93, Step 3, if desired.

A Tile Veneer
for Concrete Steps

Shaped tiles for a capped step. In laying tiles on concrete steps, first set the risers, or vertical surfaces; then set the treads, or horizontal surfaces. Always use a row of whole tile at the edge of the steps, and cut the second tiles in from the edge, if cutting is necessary. Use bull-nosé corner tiles, with two rounded edges, at the corners, and tiles with a single bullnose edge for rimming the treads and the landing.

When you are planning the tile layout for steps, leave room for a mortar joint between the riser tiles and the tread tiles, one between the riser tiles and the patio floor, and another between the top tread and the house siding.

A Flagstone-paved Patio

The roughhewn appearance and soft colors of flagstone make it an especially attractive surfacing material for patios. Limestone, sandstone, bluestone and slate are all used, sliced horizontally into slabs ¼ to ¾ inch thick. Flagstone can be lowered into a bed of sand, laid on top of a lawn, or set permanently in mortar over a concrete slab. The latter method is recommended for areas where frost, wind or rain is heavy, and for sloping sites.

Obtaining enough flagstone to cover a large area may take some looking, and buying it may be relatively expensive. In some parts of the United States and Canada flagstone is hard to find. Once you have located a source, choose each stone individually. Although part of the charm of flagstone is its irregular shapes and uneven surface, the stones should be of similar thickness—to provide a level surface for patio furniture.

When the stones are delivered, have them placed on a tarpaulin next to the slab, to prevent their sharp edges from gouging the lawn. Lay out the stones in a dry run; this lets you rearrange them for the best overall effect, and to choose which edges to cut for the best interlocking fit. Let the design dictate the width of the joints, which vary but should be in the range of ½ to 2 inches. Avoid long joint lines, if possible, and leave sizable gaps between stones to be filled later with the remnants of cut stones.

Most flagstone can be cut with a brickset and a sledge. Some varieties are soft enough to shape with just a few blows of a bricklayer's hammer, while others are so hard they need to be scored with a silicon-carbide masonry blade on a circular saw before a brickset and a hammer will break them cleanly.

After the dry run is complete, you will need to devise a system for keeping the stones in order as you lift them to prepare the mortar bed. The simplest solution is to lift them a section at a time, arranging them beside the slab in the same pattern they formed on the slab.

The setting materials for flagstone, both mortar and grout, contain more sand and are thicker than those used for clay tile. This is because the stones are heavier and the joints are wider. Although a latex additive can be used to moisten the mixture, as with tile, water works just as well. Mix a mortar of 1 part portland cement, 3 parts masonry sand and just enough water to make a stiff mixture. For the grout, mix 1 part portland cement, 1 part masonry sand, and enough water for a thick but spreadable mixture—slightly thinner than the mortar. You will also need a thick mixture of cement and water—called cement butter—as a bonding agent beneath each stone. Mix it in small quantities, to prevent it from setting before it is poured.

Flagstone, like tile, should be cleaned immediately after grouting, within 10 minutes. When the mortar and grout have cured, you may seal the joints with a masonry sealant.

Embedding Flagstones in a Matrix of Mortar

1 **Marking stones for cutting.** Arrange the flagstones over the concrete slab in a suitable pattern. Wherever a stone overlaps the edge of the slab, mark it with a pencil line, using the edge of the slab as a guide. Where one of the stones overlaps another, mark adjacent stones with interlocking cutting lines, allowing for a ½- to 2-inch joint between them. You may lay stones directly over expansion joints, if there are any. Leave all of the marked stones in place until the entire slab has been covered.

2 Cutting the stones. Remove the marked stones, one by one, and score them with a brickset and a sledge. Hold the brickset against the pencil line, and tap it several times with the sledge (*near right*); then move the brickset along the line and tap again. Continue until a breaking line has been scored across the stone. If the stone is more than 1 inch thick, score a second line on the reverse side of the stone, directly over the first. To establish this second line, extend the first line down the edges of the stone and trace a connecting line on the back.

Rest the stone on a scrap of board, the scored line overhanging the board edge slightly. Then tap the overhanging portion with the sledge until the piece snaps off (*far right*). As each stone is cut, return it to its position on the slab.

3 Seating and leveling the stones. Remove a section of stones, beginning at a corner or along an edge, and trowel on a 1-inch-thick mortar bed (*page 92, Step 1*). Then replace the stones, seating them in the mortar by tapping them with a rubber mallet. Check to make sure the stones are level. if a stone sits too high, scoop out some of the mortar from beneath it with a pointing trowel. If it sits too low, lift it and trowel more mortar into the cavity.

4 Adding cement butter. When all the stones in one section are seated, pick up each stone individually and, using a paper cup, pour about 2 ounces (several spoonfuls) of cement butter into the center of the cavity. Be sure to add equal amounts to all the stones, to preserve the even surface. Replace each stone immediately, tapping it with a rubber mallet to level the stone and bond it to the mortar.

Clear the joints between stones of any excess mortar that has pushed up between them, using a pointing trowel or a tongue depressor. Sponge excess mortar off the stones; apply grout after the mortar has cured 24 to 48 hours.

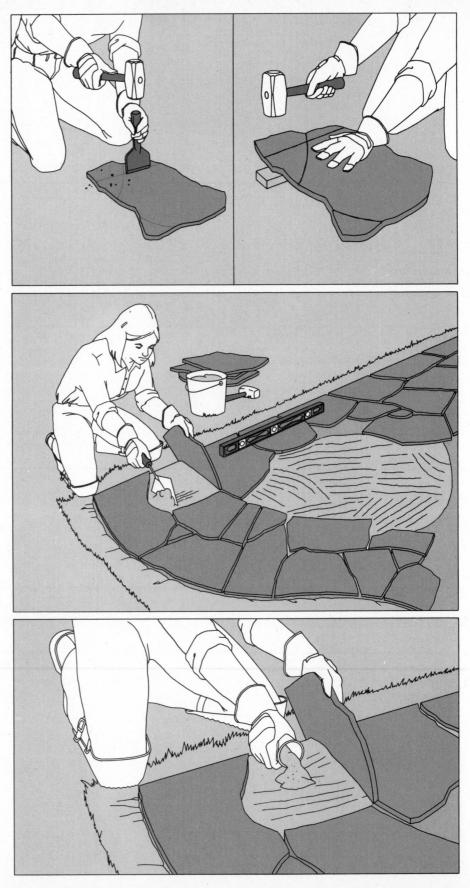

5 Grouting the joints. Apply grout along the joints with a pointing trowel. Then use the tip of a concave jointer to push the grout into the joints to a depth $\frac{1}{16}$ inch below the stone surface. Clean off any excess grout that clings to the stones. Mist the stonework every four hours for the first day, and let the grout cure three days before walking on the patio.

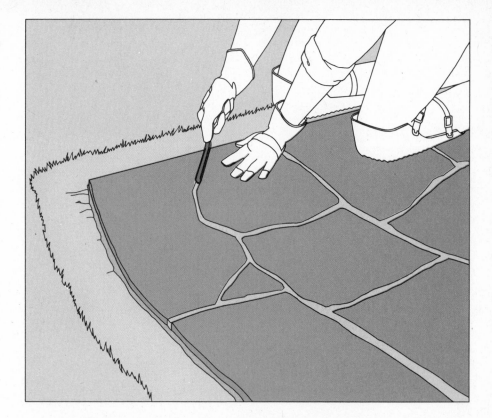

Laying Flagstone Steps

Veneering a stepped slab with stone. When cutting flagstones to fit step risers, leave space above and below the stones for mortar joints. Cut stone treads to overhang the risers by 1 inch. Plot the layout and set the stones in mortar just as for a slab *(pages 95-96, Steps 1-4),* but during the grouting process, wedge a length of 2-inch lumber against the riser to provide a temporary support for the grout in the overhanging section of the tread. After the grout has cured for three days, remove the support.

First aid for worn screens. Rejuvenating a damaged aluminum-frame screen is as easy as scribing a line. A screen-spline roller, used with flexible plastic spline, locks new screening into a channel along the edge of the frame. A convex wheel at one end of the roller creases the screening into the channel, and a concave wheel at the other end forces the spline in after it. Trim off excess screening with a utility knife, and the screen is as good as new.

"Everybody talks about the weather," observed Mark Twain, "but nobody does anything about it." Happily for owners of porches, patios and decks, this is not entirely true. Although nobody has succeeded in altering major weather patterns, people have always known how to create an agreeable microclimate for themselves—witness the fire at the mouth of the cave.

In adapting a porch, patio or deck to the vagaries of the weather, you will be dealing largely with the characteristic patterns of temperature, humidity, rainfall and wind for your locality—patterns for which the local weather bureau can supply a profile. But you may also be dealing with weather conditions specific to your site, which must be observed firsthand. If your house is on a hilltop, a patio may be buffeted by strong winds. The porch of a house in a hollow may be swathed in stagnant air—and plagued with the attendant problem of a large population of winged insects. In built-up areas, nearby structures may create wind funnels or unusual cycles of sun and shade across a deck.

Once, when houses had the luxury of many outdoor living spaces—porches, patios, gazebos—people escaped from sharp winds, hot sun or a swarm of flies by moving from one place to another. Nowadays, with limited spaces, simple baffles and screens provide the same results. A wooden framework erected over part of a deck and fitted with louvers, bamboo blinds or snow fencing will shelter the deck from the heat of the midday sun. A phalanx of windbreaks around a patio will tame blustery breezes. An enclosure of aluminum or fiberglass screening—much easier to install than copper screening—will make a porch habitable even when the summer air hangs heavy with clouds of mosquitoes.

With weather-related troubles under control, you can address yourself to making your new living space enjoyable in other ways. One desirable improvement, especially in high-density neighborhoods, is increased privacy. The overhead screen or freestanding fence that dims the sun or curbs the wind will also work to intercept the gaze of passersby and neighbors.

You will also surely want to make your new living space easily accessible. A sliding glass door will not only invite your family and friends to step outdoors onto the deck or patio but will unite indoors with out, making one an extension of the other. Finally, you will want to add furnishings appropriate to your family's outdoor activities—built-in benches to seat a crowd, a comfortable canvas sling chair for reading, a picnic table for alfresco dining. That done, your new porch, deck or patio will get maximum use—more than justifying the labor of creating it.

Adding Screens to Make a Porch Bug-proof

Screened porches call to mind balmy summer evenings, fireflies, and the gentle swish of the garden sprinkler on the lawn. But the real purpose of screens is more practical than poetic: They are meant to keep out insects. The most common screening material is 16-by-18 insect wire; the figures refer to the number of horizontal and vertical wires per square inch. This mesh is fine enough to keep out most flies and mosquitoes.

Aluminum and fiberglass are the most popular screening materials. Fiberglass, made of vinyl-coated strands of glass, is less expensive than aluminum and does not dent, scratch or corrode. But aluminum is stronger and more resistant to snagging, and it will not tear when stapled. Fiberglass solar screening, a recent development, is more densely woven and more durable than ordinary fiberglass screening. It is especially good for southern or western exposures, since it blocks up to two thirds of the sun's rays.

Aluminum screening is available in a natural bright finish, and in green and charcoal; fiberglass screening comes in these colors and several others as well. Standard widths are 24, 36, 48, 60 and 72 inches. If you are screening an entire porch, it is economical to purchase screening in 100-foot rolls from a shop that makes and repairs screens.

Any porch can be screened by one of two basic methods. The screening can be attached directly to the porch structure, or it can be framed, then set into the structure. In either case, vertical and horizontal supports are needed. The porch posts may serve as the vertical supports if they are no more than 5 feet apart; if there is a knee wall—a wall 30 to 36 inches high—the porch structure can also provide the horizontal supports.

In some cases, however, you will have to provide additional support for the screening. On a porch without a knee wall, you will have to build rectangular supporting frames, scaled to fit between existing posts. A separate framework behind the posts is required for porches where decorative columns preclude the direct attachment of screening.

To attach screening to the porch structure or to frames, you will need a staple gun and ⅜-inch copper-coated staples.

The driven staples are covered with a narrow, flat molding called screen bead; nailed on with brads, it can be pried up when the screening needs renewing.

If you build framed screens, sized to fit into openings between porch posts or in a supporting framework, each one should rest against ¾-inch molding nailed around the inside perimeter of its opening; these stops are positioned so that the frame is flush with the outside edges of the porch posts or framework.

No screened porch is complete without a screen door. A wood-frame one is easy to install and, unlike a conventional door, does not need a doorjamb. The door can be attached directly to supporting studs or porch posts with surface-mounted hinges (page 105). Hinges that have adjustable built-in springs will close the door automatically. Screen doors are available in a wide range of sizes from millwork or lumber companies. If the floor slopes across the door opening, buy a slightly taller door, to permit trimming at the bottom (page 105).

A Framework for Supporting Screening

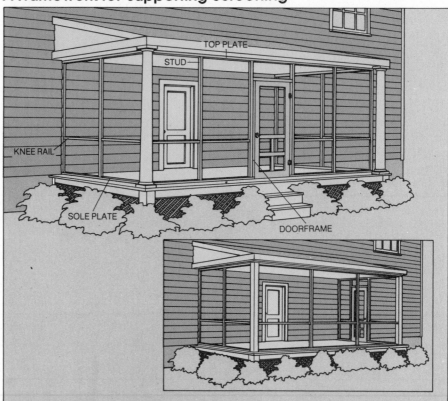

A screened porch that stands alone. Similar to a stud wall in construction, this framework is designed for a porch with decorative columns. It consists of 1-by-3 top and sole plates nailed to the ceiling and floor, plus 2-by-3 studs toe-nailed between the plates. Studs are set at each corner and spaced along the porch front and sides to make sections of equal width—no more than 5 feet if the screen is to be stapled directly to the frame, 3 feet if the frame will support removable screens. A doorframe of 2-by-3s (opposite, right) is nailed between two studs. A 1-by-3 is attached to the house wall between the top and bottom plates on each inside edge of the

porch; against clapboard siding, a notched 2-by-3 is needed (opposite, left). Horizontal 1-by-3s, nailed between the studs, form a 30-inch-high knee rail, stabilizing the framework and providing extra stapling surface. For removable screen frames, the knee rail is omitted and molding is attached to the framework (page 103, Step 5).

If the porch has posts—with flat surfaces, which are suitable for attaching screen or molding—you can build the support framework between them. Nail the top plate and the sole plate flush with the fronts of the posts, and divide the openings with 2-by-3 studs (inset).

Notching for clapboard. To seal the joint between the screening and clapboard or shingle siding, place a 2-by-3 stud against the siding between the top and sole plates. Measure the widest gap between the 2-by-3 and the siding, and set a compass to this measurement. Hold the compass so that its points are in line horizontally, with the metal tip against the siding; then move the compass vertically so that the pencil transfers the siding's profile to the 2-by-3. Cut along the jagged line with a saber saw, position the notched stud against the siding, and nail it to the house at 8-inch intervals.

A frame for a screen door. Make the doorframe with a 2-by-3 header atop two 2-by-3 jack studs, all nailed inside a pair of full-length king studs. Cut the jack studs ¾ inch shorter than the height of the screen door, because the sole plate will be removed from the doorway. Nail each jack stud to a king stud, aligning the bottom ends. Then toenail the joined pairs of studs to the top and bottom plates, jack studs facing each other, leaving an opening ¼ inch wider than the door. Cut a 2-by-3 header to fit across the frame atop the jack studs, and nail through the king studs into its ends. Saw out the sole plate between the jack studs. To keep the doorframe from twisting, use angle irons to reinforce the joints at the bottom of the frame.

TOP PLATE

HEADER

JACK STUD

KING STUD

SOLE PLATE

Framing and Installing Paneled Screens

1 Mitering the frame corners. Using a backsaw and a miter box, cut the ends of four 1-by-2s at a 45° angle, reversing the direction of the angle at each end of each piece. Make the long edge of each of the pieces ¼ inch shorter than the corresponding edge of the porch opening.

2 Joining the frame corners. Glue and fasten the angled ends together, using yellow glue and ½-inch corrugated fasteners. Drive two fasteners across the joint about 1 inch apart; then, from the other side of the frame, drive a third fastener midway between the first two.

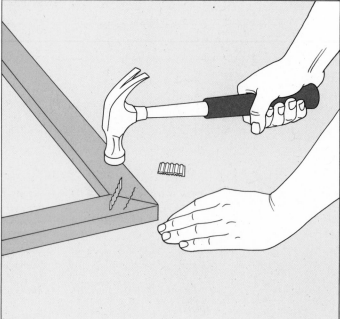

3 Stapling screening to the frame. Place the frame on a large worktable or the floor, and unroll screening over it, overlapping the edges of the frame by about 1 inch. Starting at one corner, staple the screening to one end of the frame at 2-inch intervals, positioning the staples ½ inch in from the inside edge of the frame. Pull the screening across the other end, and staple it from corner to corner, holding it taut with one hand as you staple with the other. Then staple the sides, again working from corner to corner. When all the screening is attached, use a utility knife to trim the edges about ½ inch beyond the row of staples all the way around.

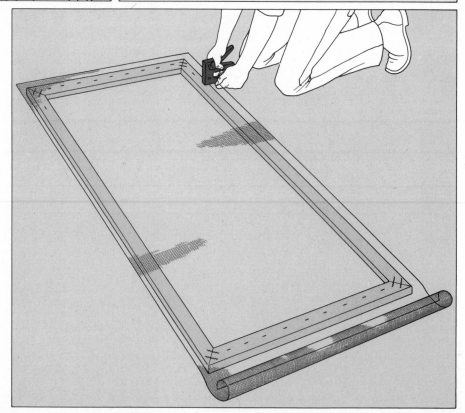

4 **Finishing the frame with lattice.** Cover the staples with 1⅜-by-¼-inch lattice strips, miter-cut to match the frame pieces. Align the outer edges of the lattice strips with the outer edges of the frame, and fasten them with ¾-inch brads driven near each edge at 6-inch intervals.

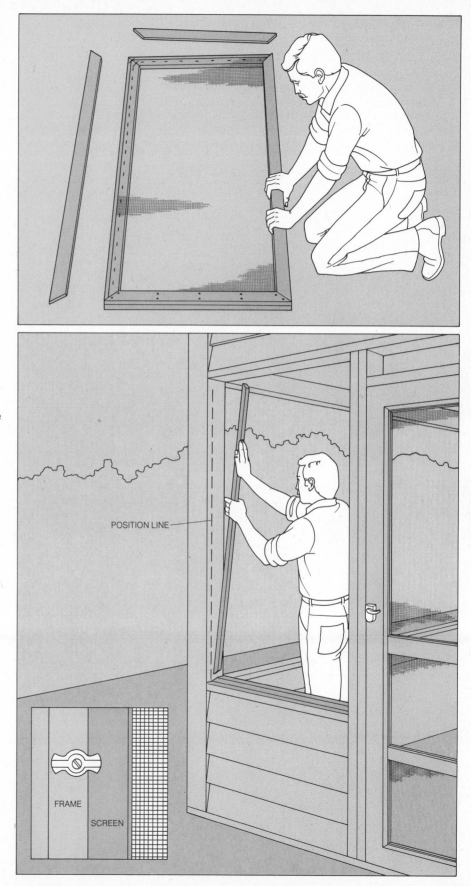

5 **Installing molding in a porch opening.** To make stops for the screen, miter-cut ¾-by-¾-inch molding strips to fit precisely along the sides, top and bottom of the porch opening. Measure the thickness of the completed screen frame, and draw a line that distance back from the outside face of all four sides of the opening. Place the molding strips along these lines, and fasten them with finishing nails every 8 inches. Position the screen against the outside of the molding; hold it in place with turn buttons (*inset*), screwed to the supporting frame so that they overlap the screens at 2-foot intervals.

POSITION LINE

FRAME

SCREEN

Attaching Screening Directly to the Porch

1 Stapling the screening. Cut a length of screening larger than the porch opening, hold it against the top of the opening, and drive a staple through each upper corner. Pull the screening taut before driving the second staple, and keep the mesh parallel with the frame. Secure the top of the screening with additional staples at 2-inch intervals, ¼ inch in from the edge of the opening. Pull the screening taut at the bottom corners, and staple the bottom in the same manner, maintaining tension by pulling the screening downward as you staple it. Staple the sides, then use a utility knife to trim away excess screening ¼ inch outside the line of staples.

2 Trimming with screen bead. Miter-cut four lengths of ⅝-inch screen bead, making the shorter edge of each piece the same length as the corresponding edge of the porch-frame opening. Position the bead over the staples, the inside edges flush with the edges of the opening. Nail the bead on with ¾-inch brads every 6 inches; to prevent warping, alternate the brads from one edge of the bead to the other.

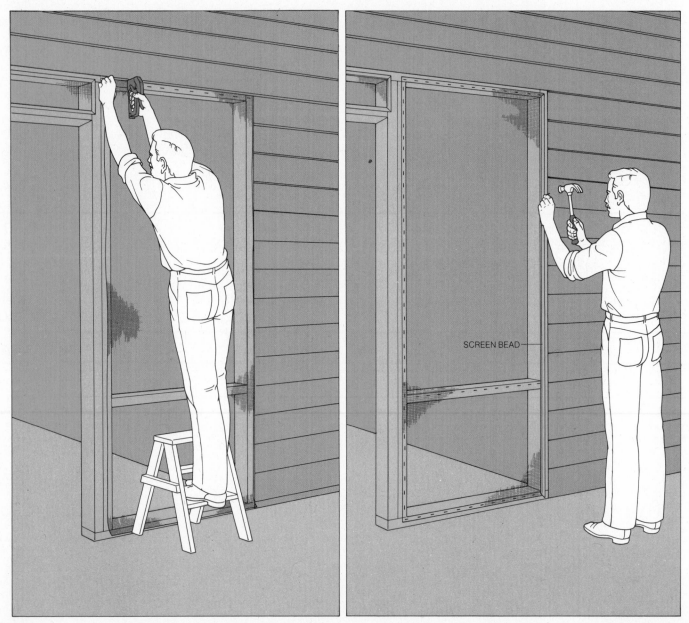

SCREEN BEAD

Hanging a Wood-Frame Screen Door

1 **Trimming the door to fit.** If the porch floor slopes across the door opening, mark and cut the bottom of the door so that it parallels the floor. To do this, have a helper hold the hinge side of the door flat against the hinge side of the frame, with one corner of the door touching the floor. Measure the gap between the floor and the door's bottom edge at the other corner; mark the same distance up from the bottom of the touching corner. Draw a line from the mark back to the first corner *(inset)*; use a plane or a saw to trim the bottom of the door along this line.

To prepare the door for hanging, attach spring hinges to the outer (hinge) side of the door, 1 foot from top and bottom. To ensure clearance between door and frame, tape two ⅛-inch-thick spacers—eightpenny common nails are ideal—on the door's edge, one above each hinge, and two more on the top near the corners.

2 **Attaching hinges to the doorframe.** Have a helper steady the door in the frame, with the spacers firmly touching the top and the hinge side of the frame and with a foot lever or shims supporting the door at the bottom. Mark the positions of holes for hinge screws on the doorframe. Take the door down, drill pilot holes, set the door back into the frame, and screw the hinges to the frame. Remove the spacers, and check the door's operation. Before installing the latch, use a block plane or a wood rasp to trim areas that bind on the latch side of the door.

NAIL SPACERS

FOOT LEVER

3 **Installing doorstop molding.** While a helper
holds the screen door closed so that it is flush with
the outside of the doorframe, use a pencil to
mark lines on the frame along the door's inside
top and sides. Cut a piece of doorstop molding
to fit the top of the frame, with 45° miters at both
ends. With the door swung open, nail this molding
to the frame so that its outside edge is flush
with the pencil line, using finishing nails at 8-inch
intervals. Cut two additional pieces of molding
the height of the frame, mitering their top ends to
fit against the upper molding, and nail them to
the sides of the frame *(inset)*.

DOORSTOP MOLDING

4 **Installing the latch.** Use the pattern provided with the latch to mark the door for a latch hole
and mounting-screw holes. Close the door and
position the pattern on the inside of the door, its
edge flush against the doorstop molding. Cut
through the pattern with a utility knife to mark the
door at the designated points. Drill holes of the
size specified in the instructions; then insert
the latch handle through the latch hole from
outside, and screw on the backplate from inside.

Establish the position for the strike plate by marking the latch-side molding at the height of the
latch. Open the door and screw the strike plate to
the doorstop molding *(inset)*.

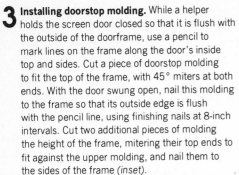

STRIKE PLATE

MOLDING

Repairing Screens and Doors

Giving a lift to a drooping door. To prevent a screen door from sagging, stretch wires with a center turnbuckle from the top of the hinge side to the bottom of the latch side. Open a 3-inch turnbuckle to nearly full extension, and attach 4 feet of woven wire to each of its eyes with a small wire clamp *(inset)*. Drive a medium-sized eye screw into the door's face about 2 inches from the top corner of the hinge side, and attach one free end of wire to the eye screw with a wire clamp. Drive another eye screw about 2 inches from the bottom corner of the latch side, pull the other wire through, and hold the wire taut as you attach a wire clamp. Turn the center section of the turnbuckle, with pliers if necessary, tightening the wires to hold the door square.

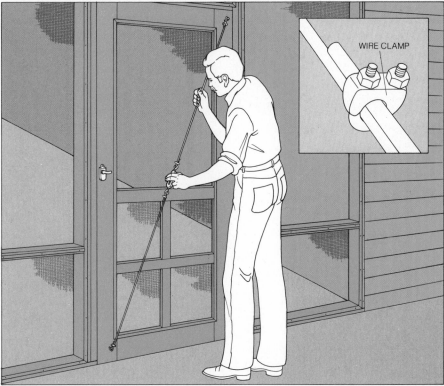

WIRE CLAMP

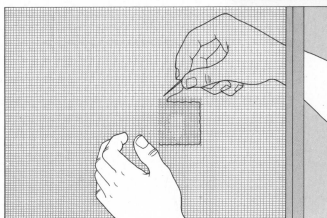

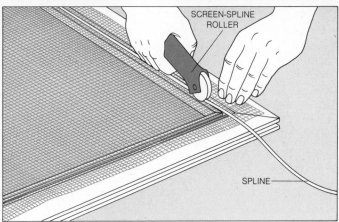

SCREEN-SPLINE ROLLER

SPLINE

Patching an aluminum screen. To repair a small hole in an aluminum screen, cut away ragged edges, then use a needle and nylon thread to sew on a patch. Cut the patch from matching screening, overlapping the hole by ½ inch on all sides. Hold the patch over the hole and use a sewing needle to weave nylon monofilament sewing thread through both the screen and the patch, ¼ inch from the edge of the patch, passing through each square of mesh. When you have woven all around, weave a second border ⅛ inch from the edge. End this border about ½ inch past the starting point of the first.

If you cannot reach both sides of the hole at the same time, have a helper on the opposite side of the screen return the needle on each stitch, or use a curved upholstery needle and make at least three passes around the patch.

New screening for an aluminum frame. Remove damaged screening by pulling the flexible vinyl spline out of the channel around the edge; then cut a new piece of screening that will overlap the spline channel an inch on each side. If you are using aluminum screening, crease it into the channel with a screen-spline roller; this is not necessary with fiberglass screening.

Position a length of spline over the screening at one end of the frame, and use the roller to force the spline and screening into the channel, keeping the screen mesh parallel with the frame. Trim away excess spline at the corners. Install spline at the opposite end, pulling the screening taut as you work. Then install lengths of spline in the same manner in the side channels. Use a utility knife to trim excess screening flush with the outer edge of the spline.

Coverings That Modulate the Sun's Rays

Adding an overhead covering to a patio or deck serves two purposes: It increases the usefulness of the outdoor living space by shielding it from the sun, and it helps to integrate the deck or patio with the architecture of the house. The covering can be a leafy bower, a canvas awning lashed to a wood-and-pipe frame, a simple arrangement of snow fencing unrolled on top of cleats, or a permanent structure of sun-filtering wooden louvers.

The choice of covering depends largely on orientation and ventilation. If the deck or patio faces south and is heated by daylong sun, you may want the solid shade of a canvas awning, installed as described on pages 114-115, or of plastic panels, predrilled, then nailed to a wood frame. On the other hand, ventilation can be a concern: If a solid covering is to be attached to two or more house walls, hot air can build up underneath it. A covering that lets air circulate—such as louvers, an eggcrate grid or even split bamboo—could be a better choice.

For a deck or patio that receives sun during only part of the day, a covering that offers partial shade is generally sufficient. The 24-inch eggcrate grid shown on page 112 supplies some shade, especially in the midmorning and midafternoon. It can also serve as the basis for a denser covering of 2-by-2 slats, spaced at whatever intervals and in whatever configuration you choose. On page 112, the slats are placed at right angles in alternate grids for a checkerboard pattern. Snow fencing is a quick-and-easy covering for dappled shade, as is woven-reed fencing or blinds of split bamboo. Their life expectancy is short, but all three are easily and inexpensively replaced.

More effective than any of these in regulating the amount of sun that reaches the deck or patio are louvers. Mounted on a north-south axis, they can be oriented to the east, to admit sunlight in the morning and block the hotter afternoon rays. Slanting the louvers to the west reverses the effect. Placing the louvers on an east-west axis, slanting them to the north, will deflect the midday sun of summer but admit some morning and evening sunlight. Whatever the orientation, louvers are generally set at an angle of 40° to 50°.

In choosing a covering, you will also want to weigh its effect on the interior of the house. A covering that creates dense shade reduces the amount of the sun's light and warmth in the house, a boon in summer but not in winter. You may prefer a cover that is removable in winter, such as one of canvas or split bamboo, or you may choose shade from a deciduous vine such as grape or wisteria, which will lose its leaves in winter.

As for any construction project, plan your cover with care. Use standard-dimension lumber, treated to resist decay, in sizes suited to the spans and to the weight of the covering material. The local building department can usually advise you on safe spans for the lumber sizes you propose to use. Generally 4-by-4 lumber, in lengths from 8 to 12 feet, is acceptable for posts. The distance a beam can span is determined by its width: A 2-by-6 beam is typically supported by posts spaced no more than 6 feet apart, a 2-by-8 beam by posts no more than 8 feet apart. Similarly, 2-by-6 rafters, spaced 24 inches center to center, span distances of up to 10 feet; 2-by-8s are often needed for 12-foot spans and 2-by-10s for spans of up to 16 feet.

These spans, incorporated in the 8-by-10-foot structure illustrated here can be used to support various types of covers. They will bear a moderate snow load of 20 pounds per square foot; if you live in an area of heavy snow or no snow, you should consult your local building department or structural engineer for appropriate modifications. This framework is designed to be attached to a wood-floored deck, but you can adapt it for use on a concrete patio by anchoring the posts to the slab using post anchors and lead shields. Or the posts can be set on concrete footings (page 33).

Before starting the actual construction, you may want to cut decorative ends on beams and rafters. These give a professional touch to the finished structure.

Putting Up the Structural Support

1 Positioning a ledger on the house. To establish the location of the ledger, the board that will hold rafters to the house, measure from the ceiling to the top of the doorway, inside the house, and transfer this measurement to the exterior at each end of the doorway. Using these marks as reference points, snap a level chalk line above the door. With a helper, rest the lower edge of a 2-by-6 ledger, 8 feet 4 inches long, on this line, centered over the doorway, and nail the ledger in place temporarily to mark holes for lag screws. Then drill holes for the screws and attach it permanently (*pages 12-13*).

Cut two 4-by-4 posts long enough to reach from a point level with the bottom of the ledger to the bottom of the ribbon board underneath the deck. Position the posts along the outer edge of the deck to align with a point 2 inches in from each end of the ledger. Secure the posts to the ribbon with 6-inch-long ½-inch carriage bolts (*inset*). To position the beam, draw a horizontal line 7¼ inches below the top of each post on the sides facing toward and away from the house.

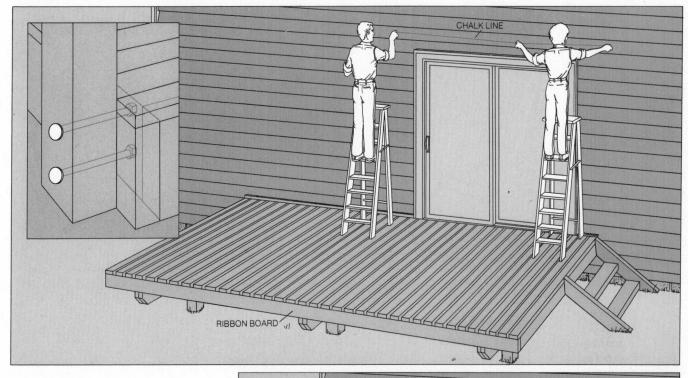

CHALK LINE

RIBBON BOARD

2 Attaching the beam. With a helper, lift a 10-foot-long 2-by-8 beam and hold it against the outside of the posts, positioning it so that it extends 1 foot beyond the posts, with its lower edge at the 7¼-inch lines. Check the beam to be sure it is level, then secure it temporarily to each post with an eightpenny (2½-inch) nail. Repeat to attach a second 2-by-8 beam to the inner side of the posts. Using an 8-inch-long ½-inch bit, drill two holes through each post-and-beam assembly, and secure the assembly with ½-inch carriage bolts and washers (*inset*). Cut seven 4-by-4 spacers, each 7 inches long, and nail them between the beams at 1-foot intervals.

Draw a vertical line 2¾ inches in from each end of the ledger. Then subdivide the distance between these two lines with three additional lines spaced 23½ inches apart. Center and nail a 6-inch metal joist hanger over each line. Mark identically spaced lines on top of the beams, placing the first pair of vertical lines ¾ inch in from the outer face of each post.

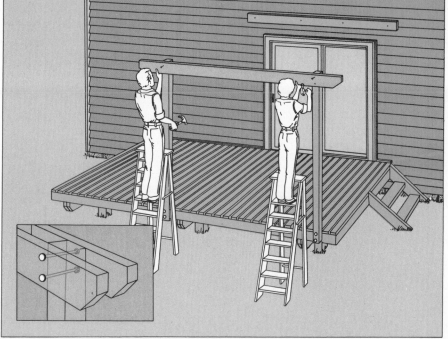

3 Placing the rafters. Cut five 2-by-6 rafters, each 11 feet 3½ inches long, and rest the outer end of each one atop one of the lines marked on the beams. Fit the inner end into a joist hanger, and nail it in place. At the beam end, toe-nail the rafter into both sides of the beam, using two tenpenny (3-inch) nails on each side. Continue until all the rafters are in place.

Constructing a Sun Screen of Slanted Louvers

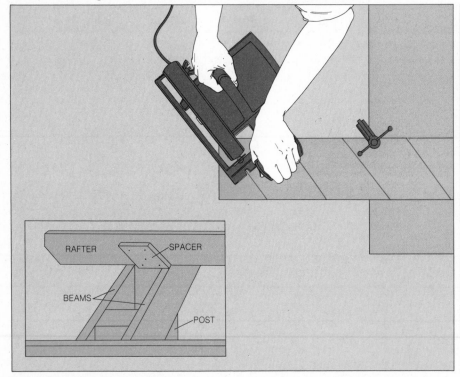

RAFTER SPACER

BEAMS

POST

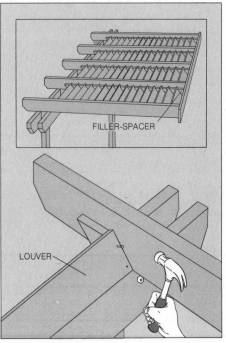

FILLER-SPACER

LOUVER

1 Cutting the spacers. With a protractor or a T bevel, mark a length of 1-by-4 lumber with a series of parallel lines angled at 50°, spacing the lines 4 inches apart. Then cut along the lines with a circular saw. For the 8-by-10 structure that is shown on the preceding pages, you will need approximately 100 pairs of spacers, requiring about 70 feet of lumber.

Nail the first pair of spacers to the beam ends of two facing rafters. In the example shown, it is assumed that the deck is on the east side of the house and the goal is to admit morning sun

but provide afternoon shade. For this result, set the bottom edges of the spacers flush with the bottom edges of the rafters, and set the spacers so that their downward slant runs toward the house. The inner edges of the spacers should meet the rafter bottoms at the point where the rafters cross the inner face of the beam *(inset)*.

For decks or patios oriented in other directions, different louver configurations may be needed; for example, if your deck faces south, slanting the louvers toward the north will provide maximum shade in the late afternoon.

2 Installing the louvers. Cut a 1-by-6 louver that will fit between the two rafters, and lay it against the first pair of spacers; nail the louver to the edges of the spacers. Then nail a second pair of spacers to the rafters, and attach a second louver. Continue adding spacers and louvers until the entire row has been filled. When the last louver has been nailed into place, measure the distances from the bottom of the louver and the top of the louver to the ledger; then, using these measurements to determine the shape needed, cut a pair of filler-spacers. Nail the filler-spacers into place. Repeat this assembly process of spacers and louvers between each pair of rafters *(inset)*.

Making Panels of Woven Reed

1 **Installing support cleats.** To support panels of woven-reed fencing, nail 1-by-2 cleats along the lower edge of each rafter. Make the cleats long enough to extend from the inner face of the beam to the joist hanger.

Cut four pieces of 2-by-2 to frame each reed panel, making two pieces 22½ inches long, the other two 57 inches long. Glue and nail the shorter endpieces across the ends of the longer sidepieces. Construct eight such frames.

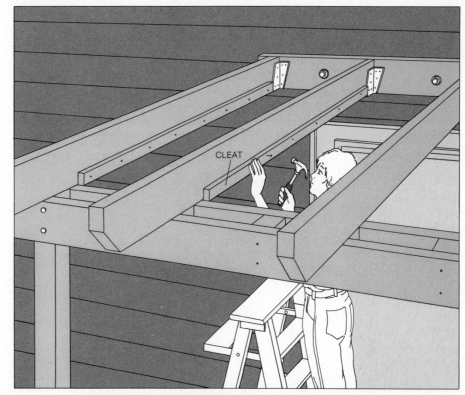

2 **Attaching reed.** Lay woven-reed fencing, available at garden-supply stores, across the width of the wood frame, fastening it to the frame on all edges with ½-inch copper-coated staples spaced 2 inches apart. Trim off excess fencing with a saber saw. Repeat for each frame. Lower the frames into place, allowing them to rest loosely atop the cleats (inset).

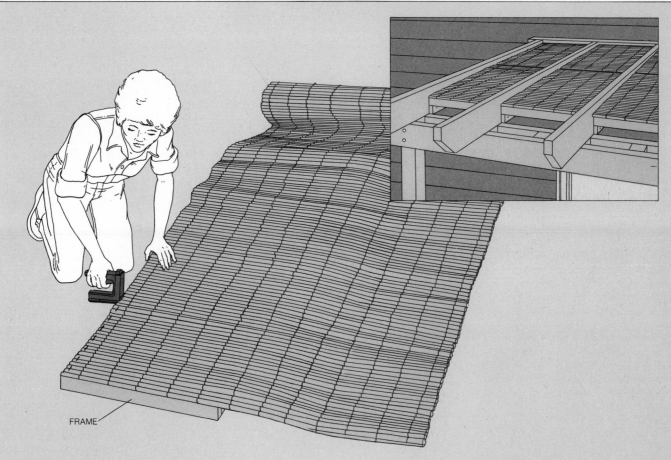

Coverings for Varying Degrees of Shade

An airy eggcrate. Mark the bottoms of the two outer rafters at 24-inch intervals, beginning 24 inches from the ledger board. Snap a chalk line between the pairs of marks, to transfer the measurements to intervening rafters. Using a steel square, transfer these marks to the vertical faces of each rafter. Cut 2-by-6 crosspieces to fit between the rafters at the marks, and between the rafters above the middle of the beam. Nail each crosspiece to its rafters; butt-nail one end and toenail the other (*inset*), using tenpenny (3-inch) galvanized finishing nails. Set the nails.

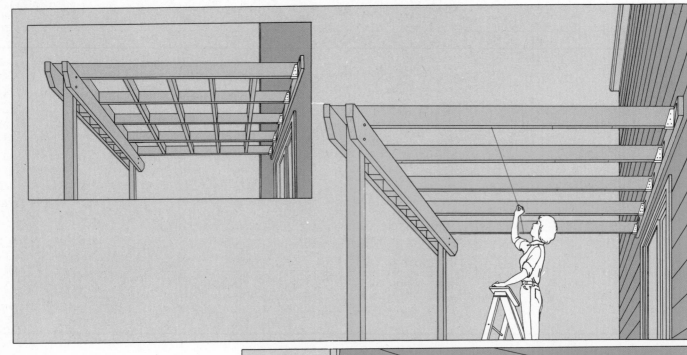

A checkerboard grid for deeper shade. Using the eggcrate covering (*above*) as a base, top each square with eight 2-by-2s, cut 24 inches long. Begin working at a corner square at either end of the ledger board, placing the first 2-by-2 across two rafters, its ends at the midpoint of the edge of the rafters. Center the second 2-by-2 between the rafters at the opposite end of the square, aligning its outer edge with the midpoint of the crosspiece. Fill the intervening area with six more 2-by-2s, spaced at even intervals. Nail the boards to the rafters, using two eightpenny (2½-inch) finishing nails at each end of each board.

On an adjacent square, reverse the direction of the 2-by-2s so that they run across two crosspieces. Continue in this fashion, changing the direction of the 2-by-2s on adjacent squares to create a checkerboard pattern (*inset*).

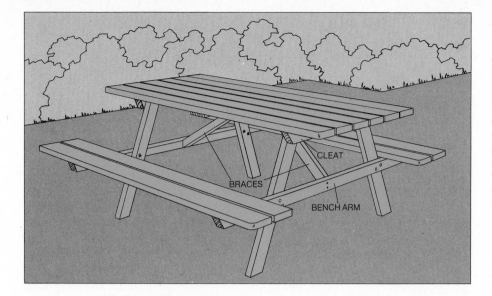

A One-Piece Picnic Table

Anatomy of a picnic table. This traditional 3-by-7-foot trestle table with two integral benches is made of 2-by-4 and 2-by-6 boards. The 2-by-6s that form the tabletop are held together underneath by three 2-by-4 cleats. Fastened to the end cleats are two pairs of 2-by-4 legs, which are crossed by two 2-by-4 arms that support the 2-by-6 planks of the seats. For added stability, diagonal 2-by-4 braces run from the center cleat to the bench arms. The entire structure is fastened together with galvanized bolts and wood screws.

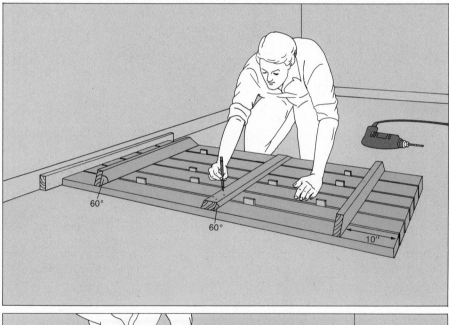

Putting the Parts Together

1 Assembling the tabletop. On a flat surface, lay out six 2-by-6 planks, 7 feet long, bracing their ends against a straight, rigid support. Set ¼-inch spacers between the boards. Cut three 2-by-4 cleats 34 inches long, mitering the ends at opposing 60° angles; miter two of the cleats on edge and set them 10 inches in from the ends of the tabletop; miter the third cleat flat and set it across the center. Mark screw positions—two for each plank—in a zig-zag pattern on the middle cleat, in a straight line on each end cleat.

Fasten the cleats to the top, drilling pilot holes for 2¾-inch screws at the marks. On the end cleats, drill a 2-inch countersink hole in one edge and a pilot hole in the other; to match the holes, draw a squared guideline around the cleat and bisect the line on each edge.

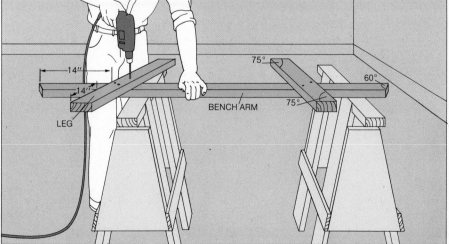

2 Joining the legs and bench arms. Cut two bench arms 64 inches long, and four legs 32 inches long, from 2-by-4 lumber. Miter the ends of the bench arms at opposite 60° angles, and the ends of the legs at parallel 75° angles. Measure along the longer edge of each bench arm, 14 inches in from both ends, and mark a 75° angle slanted in the opposite direction from the nearest mitered end. Tack the table legs to the bench arms just inside these marks, positioning each leg so that its outside edge extends 14 inches below the bench arm. Drill two ⅜-inch holes, diagonal to each other, through each leg and the bench arm. Insert a 3½-inch carriage bolt through each hole, bolthead on the bench-arm side, and fasten the legs to the bench arms.

3 **Fastening the legs to the cleats.** Clamp the top of a leg assembly to the inside of an end cleat so that the legs are equal distances from the edges of the tabletop, and drill two ⅜-inch holes, diagonally spaced, through the cleat and each leg. Fasten the legs to the cleats with 3½-inch carriage bolts, boltheads on the cleat side.

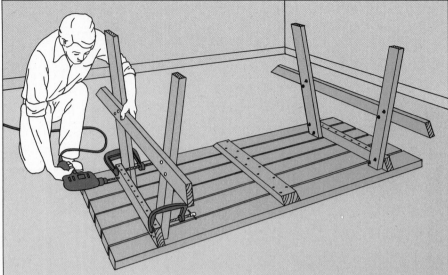

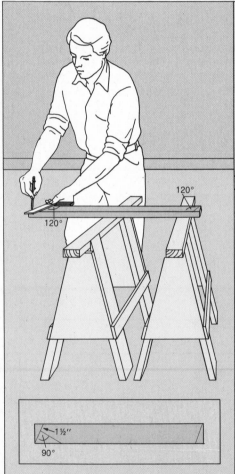

CLEAT

BENCH ARM

4 **Installing diagonal braces.** Cut two 2-by-4s 33½ inches long. Using a T bevel set at 120°, mark parallel lines to form angles at both ends of each board (*above, left*). Then, at one end of each board, measure in 1½ inches from the apex of the 120° angle along the slanted line; from there extend a second line, perpendicular to the first, to the edge of the board (*inset*). Cut the boards along the marked lines. Butt the double-cut end of each brace against the midpoint of the center cleat; butt the other end of each brace against a bench arm. Using tenpenny (3-inch) nails, toenail the sides of the braces into the center cleat and the tabletop. Then nail through the bench arms into the ends of the braces (*above, right*).

Add seats by laying two 2-by-6 boards across the bench-arm extensions, spacing the boards ¼ inch apart. Drive tenpenny nails through the boards into the bench arms.

Plastic Furniture from Lightweight Tubing

Three all-purpose plastic pieces. The chair, footstool and side table shown here are all made of schedule-40 PVC (plastic) pipe—1½-inch pipe for the chair, 1-inch pipe for the footstool and table. They are joined with cross, elbow and T fittings of the same material. The measurements given for each pipe section are based on standard sizes for the three pieces of furniture, but the sizes may vary to suit your needs. When calculating pipe lengths, subtract the length of the connecting fitting but add the depth of the fitting socket at each end of the pipe. When two fittings butt together, join them with a piece of pipe equal in length to two socket depths.

On the chair and footstool, canvas slings, sewn to fit around horizontal crosspieces, support removable cushions. The two-piece sling for the seat and back of the chair is stitched together at a line 7 inches from the back crosspiece.

Joining pipes and fittings. Cut all pipe sections at once, using the measurements given in the drawings above, and fit the parts together loosely in a dry run. Work on a flat surface so that parallel joints are in alignment and perpendicular joints are square. For a chair, assemble the side sections first, then add the crosspieces for the seat and back. When the piece is complete, use a utility knife to scratch a guideline across the pipe and fitting at each joint *(inset);* the marks will speed reassembly as you glue the parts together. Disassemble the parts.

Working in a well-ventilated area and following the same sequence used in the dry run, glue all the parts together except the crosspieces that support the canvas slings. Spread pipe cement on the inner lip of each fitting and slip the pipe into the fitting, tapping it with a rubber mallet if necessary for a snug fit. Hold each joint together for 30 seconds, until the glue has set. Attach the crosspieces for the canvas sling last, but do not glue them. Drill pilot holes through an inconspicuous spot on each joint, and screw the joints together with ½-inch wood screws, so that they can be taken apart and the canvas slings removed for washing.

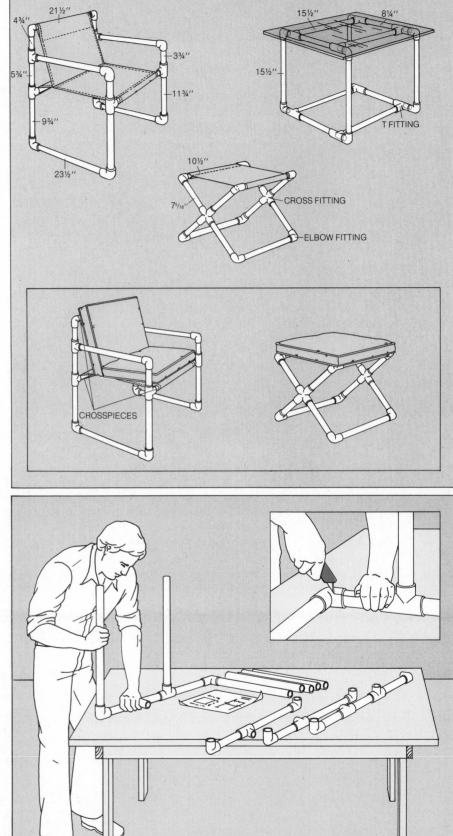

Picture Credits

The sources for the illustrations in this book are shown below. The drawings were created by Jack Arthur, Laszlo Bodrogi, Roger Essley, Charles Forsythe, John Jones, Dick Lee, John Martinez and Joan McGurren. Credits for the illustrations from left to right are separated by semicolons, from top to bottom by dashes.

Cover: Fil Hunter. 6: Fil Hunter. 9-17: John Massey. 18-23: Eduino J. Pereira from Arts & Words. 24-29: Walter Hilmers Jr. from HJ Commercial Art. 30-43: Frederic F. Bigio from B-C Graphics. 44-47: Snowden Associates, Inc. 49, 50: ©Robert Perron, 1980. 51: Dudley Witney—Stephen Brown. 52: Bradley Olman—Dudley Witney. 53: Norman McGrath. 54: Ezra Stoller ©ESTO, George van Geldern, architect. 55: Dudley Witney—Robert Lautman, Anthony Ruddy, SunCraft Deck Designs, Inc. 56: ©1980 Enrico Ferorelli, designed by Mrs. Charles Fairchild Fuller. 57: Library of Congress. 58: Fil Hunter. 61-67: Ray Skibinski. 68-73: Terry Atkinson from Arts & Words. 74-77: Walter Hilmers Jr. from HJ Commercial Art. 78, 79: Gerry Gallagher. 81-87: John Massey. 88-97: William J. Hennessy. 98: Fil Hunter. 100-107: Frederic F. Bigio from B-C Graphics. 109-115: James Anderson. 116-119: John Massey. 120-127: Walter Hilmers Jr. from HJ Commercial Art. 128-133: Elsie J. Hennig.

Acknowledgments

The index/glossary for this book was prepared by Louise Hedberg. The editors also wish to thank the following: Roslyn and Stuart Addison, Coconut Creek, Fla.; American Wood Preservers Institute, McLean, Va.; Dennis A. Baker, Alexandria, Va.; Glen C. Baker, Contractor, Alexandria, Va.; Jack Blevins, Annandale, Va.; Donald G. Buckingham, Washington Canopies, Inc., Bladensburg, Md.; Scott Dennison, Blaine Window Repair Service, Kensington, Md.; Discount Window Service, Rockville, Md.; John Dudley, C. E. Cornwell Construction Co., Manassas, Va.; Kurt Duesterdick, Poolservice Co., Arlington, Va.; Inger and Osborn Elliott, New York, N.Y.; Mr. and Mrs. R. Sherrard Elliot, Jr., Alexandria, Va.; William Faulkenberry, Brick Institute of America, McLean, Va.; Dr. and Mrs. Herb Galloway, Atlanta, Ga.; Col. and Mrs. Joseph Garbacz, Alexandria, Va.; Gregory Green, Alexandria, Va.; Kathlyn Hatch, Boston, Mass.; Mark A. Hefley, Turncraft, White City, Ore.; Donald H. Johnson, Somerset Door & Column Co., Somerset, Pa.; Robert W. Johnson, Virginia Roofing Corp., Alexandria, Va.; Daniel E. Linaugh, Brick Shoppe, Inc., Rockville, Md.; Luck Stone Center, Sterling, Va.; Jess McIlvain, Architectural Director, Tile Council of America, Washington, D.C.; Eileen McLaughlin, Spring Lake Historical Society, Spring Lake, N.J.; Richard C. Meininger, National Ready Mixed Concrete Association, Silver Spring, Md.; The Mosaic Tile Company of Virginia, Newington, Va.; Cintra Murray, Coatesville, Pa.; Denys Peter Myers, Architectural Historian, Alexandria, Va.; Frank Plombon, Home, Inc., Arlington, Va.; Stephen K. Powell, PAR Construction Corp., Merrifield, Va.; Richard Ridley, Washington, D.C.; James H. Roper, Managing Editor, *American Preservation*, Little Rock, Ark.; Stephen Schuyler, Betco Block and Products, Inc., Bethesda, Md.; Ralph Spears, Portland Cement Association, Skokie, Ill.; Rick Spitzmiller, Architectural Consultant, Historic Savannah Foundation, Savannah, Ga.; Elizabeth Sporkin, Chevy Chase, Md.; Alicia Stamm, National Architectural & Engineering Record, Washington, D.C.; Carole and Robert Testwuide, Oakton, Va.; Catharine S. Trimble, Westchester, Pa.; United States Army Corps of Engineers, Concrete Section, Directorate of Civil Works, Washington, D.C.; Paul Wahler, Poolservice Co., Arlington, Va.; Brian Whittier, Fredericksburg, Va.; Robert Wilde, Executive Director, American Concrete Institute, Detroit, Mich.; Roger Williams Jr., Stonington Historical Society, Stonington, Conn. The editors also thank Edgar Henry, Wendy Murphy and Kirk Y. Saunders, writers, for their help with this book.

Index/Glossary

Included in this index are definitions of many of the technical terms used in this book. Page references in italics indicate an illustration of the subject mentioned.

Air-entraining agent: *chemical added to concrete mix that keeps it from cracking in cold climates.* Use, 68

Basket-weave: *pattern of laid bricks.* Shown, *81*

Bell jack: *tool used to support low decks or porch floors.* Using, 44

Benches: anchoring posts in concrete, *130;* building into railings of deck or porch, *128-129;* curved, *130;* for picnic table, *131-132*

Bleed water: *moisture in concrete that must evaporate before finish is applied.* Described, 68, 70, 71, 72

Bricks: in cold climates, 80; common, 80, *81;* cutting with a brickset, *84;* cutting with a circular saw, *84;* edging, 80, *82;* face, 80, *81;* filling joints between 80, *86;* herringbone pattern, *81, 84;* interlocking pavers, *58, 81;* laying over sand, 80, *81-85;* mortar for, 80, *86;* orienting the pattern, 80; patterns, *81;* paving bricks, 80, *81;* paving a concrete slab, 80, *86;* in porch piers, 8, *11-12;* removing moss and weeds, 80; scalloped pattern, *81, 85;* set in a circle around a tree, *81, 83;* veneering concrete steps, *87*

Canvas sun screen: attaching, *114-115*

Carriages: *notched boards supporting stairs.* Attaching to porch, 9, *17;* cutting, *16*

Cement butter: *thick mix of cement and water.* Bonding with, 95, 96

Chair: made of PVC pipe, *128, 133*

Column: adding, *29;* removing a solid porch column, *44-45;* repairing a hollow column, 44, *45*

Concrete: curing, 68; mixing, 68; ordering, 68; paving blocks, *73;* for porch footings, 8; for slab, 60, *61*

Concrete footing: anchoring posts in, 44, *45;* for bench posts, *130;* for brick piers, 8, 9, *10-11;* building up, as base for new post, *46;* for concrete steps, *74, 87;* and risers, for steps on a slope, *74, 77;* setting deck posts in, *33-34;* for windbreak, 116

Concrete slab: calculating amounts of gravel and concrete needed, *chart 60,* *61;* curing, 68; edging, *70;* excavating and grading, 59, *61-63,* 66; expansion joint, 60, *62, 64, 65, 67,* 69; filling small cracks and holes, 78; finishing surface, *70-71;* flagstone effect, *71;* form boards, 60, *63, 65-66, 67;* free-form, *61, 66-67;* gravel drainage bed, 60, *64, 67;* greasing forms, 68; patching, *78-79;* pavers, *73;* paving with stone, *95-97;* pebble-aggregate surface, 68, *71-72;* planning, 59, 60, *61;* pouring and finishing, *68-73;* rectangular, 59, 60, *61-66;* redwood in, *72-73;* screeding, *69;* site for, 60; skidproof surface, *71;* slope of, 60; smoothing, *69;* testing surface, 78; tiling, *88-94;* veneering with brick, 80, *86*

Deck, 7, *30;* alternative designs, *40-41, 43;* anchoring platforms, *31-33;* angling corners, *40-41;* beam, *30, 31-32;* boards, *30, 35-36;* building benches into railing, *128-129;* canvas awning, *114-115;* decking patterns, *36;* eggcrate grid, *112;* footings, *30, 33-34;* framework for sun screen, *108, 109-110;* hanging joists, *30, 31-32;* jacking up to repair posts, *45-46;* louvered sun screen, *110;* posts, *30, 34;* railings, *30, 37-39, 41-42;* ribbon board, *30, 31-32;* snow fencing, *113;* stairs, *30, 40;* training vines to cover, *113;* wood for, 30. *See also* Outdoor furniture

Decking: boards for, 30; diagonal and herringbone patterns, *36;* nailing down, *35;* trimming, *35*

Doors: screen, framing and hanging, *100, 101, 105-106, 107;* sliding glass, *120-127*

Eggcrate-grid sun screen, *108, 112;* supporting framework, *109-110;* training vines to grow over, *113*

Expansion joint: *joint between concrete slabs.* And brick, 80, 87; laying stones over, 95; laying tile over, *92, 93;* positioning in slab, *62, 64, 65, 67,* 69

Fiberglass solar screening, 100

Flagstone: arranging, *95;* choosing stones, 95; cutting, 95, *96;* grouting, *97;* sealing joints, 95; setting in mortar, 95, *96-97;* veneering steps, *97*

Floorboards, tongue-and-groove: laying on porch, 7, 8, 9, *15;* replacing, *47;* treating, 8

Framing square: marking carriages with, *16;* marking joists, *13;* roofer's,

18, 19, *21-24*

Frost line: *deepest level frost penetrates soil.* And depth of footings, 9

Grout: curing, *93, 97;* edging tiled slab, *94;* filling joints between ceramic tiles, 88, *92-93;* for stone, 95, 97

Herringbone: decking pattern, *36;* pattern of laid bricks, *81, 84*

Insects and insect damage: signs of, 44

Jack-on-jack: *pattern of laying bricks.* Shown, *81*

Jacks: bell, 44; house, 44, *45;* jacking deck or porch floor, *45-46;* jacking porch roof, 6, *44-45*

Joists: deck, *30, 31-32;* hanging, for porch floor, 8, 9, *13-14;* load, 8, 12; on porch roof, *18, 19;* reinforcing weak, *46;* span of, *chart* 12; wood for, 12

Lattice screen, *17*

Louvered sun screen, *108;* building, *110;* orientation, 108, 110; supporting framework for, *109-110*

Maintenance: treating wood, 44; of wood porches and decks, 44

Moisture: protecting inside of porch column, 29; signs of rot, 44

Mortar: in brick piers, 8; for building or face bricks, 80, *86;* laying bricks in, *86;* for outdoor use, 80; for step veneering, *87;* for stone, 95, *96-97;* for tiles, 88, *92-94*

Mosaic tiles, 88, *89*

Muriatic acid, 86

Outdoor furniture: benches built into deck railing, *128-129;* building a curved bench, *130;* chairs and tables made of PVC pipe, *128, 133;* trestle-type picnic table with two benches, *131-132;* wood for, 128

Paint, maintaining on porch or deck, 44

Patio, 7; circular, *81, 83;* digging and pouring a concrete slab, *61-73;* and flagstone, *95-97;* furniture for, 128, *130-133;* grading and preparing site, 59, 60; laying out a sand bed, 80, *82-85;* masonry, 59, *60-97;* paving with brick, 80, *81-86;* paving with concrete, 60, *61-79;* scalloped pattern, *81, 85;* setting tile in mortar, 88, *92-94;* sliding glass door,

135